The B Jelly Rolls
Non-Fattening
Sugar Free
No Cholesterol

Yardage is Given for:
Either 5" 'Charm Squares',
'Jelly Roll' 2½" strips
OR fabric yardage.

Index

Daydreams
pages 4 - 5

Red, White and Bold
pages 8 - 9

A Morris Garden
pages 6 - 7

Kashmir
page 10

Prairie Paisley
page 45

Through the Garden Gate
'Block of the Month'
pages 46 - 47

Swell Quilt
page 49

Swell Baby & Toddler – Girl and Boy
pages 48 - 49

Flutterby
pages 50 - 51

Simply Strips & Squares 3

Daydreams Squares

Butterflies flit across the borders of a fairyland made of chocolate and cherries.

instructions on pages 16 - 17

Daydreams Strips Dramatic Setting

*pieced by Donna Perrotta
quilted by Julie Lawson*

Log Cabin blocks are a traditional favorite with novice and experienced quilters alike because they are simple to construct and offer a variety of design possibilities when setting the blocks together.

A touch of mint and soft aqua balances this dramatic setting.

instructions on pages 13 - 15

Simply Strips & Squares 5

6 *Simply Strips & Squares*

A Morris Garden Squares Wall Quilt

pieced by Donna Perrotta
quilted by Sue Needle

Inspired by the work of the influential British artist, designer, and poet William Morris, these fabrics reproduce the layers of complex repeats, intertwining leaves, and curving stems that characterize the natural inspirations of Art Nouveau.

instructions on pages 18 - 19

A Morris Garden Log Cabin Window Blocks

pieced by Kayleen Allen
quilted by Julie Lawson

Capture the look of sunny windows set in colors and patterns influenced by nature.

William Morris sketched the plants in his own garden and preferred intricate lines and elegant curves. His art is reproduced beautifully in this exquisite fabric collection.

instructions on pages 20 - 21

Simply Strips & Squares 7

Red, White, and Bold Charms Quilt

pieced by Donna Perrotta quilted by Julie Lawson

Brimming with American pride, this red, white and blue wall hanging makes a bold statement that fits into the small, bare spaces of your home or office.

Patriotism is never out of style, so this great piece blends with any decor all year long

instructions on pages 22 - 23

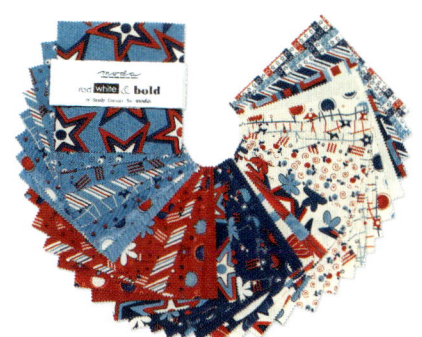

Red White & Bold Strips Squares in Squares

pieced by Donna Perrotta quilted by Julie Lawson

Red hot and bold, this quilt appeals to all ages.

Everyone in the family is going to want this quilt on their bed or favorite chair, and it's so easy to construct, you may be inclined to make two.

instructions on pages 24 - 25

Simply Strips & Squares 9

Kashmir
pieced by Donna Perrotta
quilted by Julie Lawson
Immerse yourself in rich textures, ornate printed patterns, and sumptuous colors with a fun pinwheel design.

instructions on pages 11 - 12

Kashmir

photo is on page 10

SIZE: 44" x 52"

YARDAGE:
We used *Moda* "Kashmir II" by Sentimental
   Studios - we purchased 3 Charm Packs
   (You'll need a total of 76 squares 5" x 5")
   6 Red   OR   1/6 yard
   6 Olive   OR   1/6 yard
   6 Blue   OR   1/6 yard
   6 Blue-Gray   OR   1/6 yard
   4 Light Green   OR   1/6 yard
   4 Goldish (3 Gold-1 Green)   OR   1/6 yard
   24 Cream/Lt Prints   OR   1/2 yard
   20 Assorted (Green-Blue-Grey) OR   1/2 yard

Border #1   Purchase 1/3 yard Olive Green print
Border #2 & Binding
             Purchase 1 1/8 yards Green print
Backing   Purchase 2 yards
Batting   Purchase 52" x 60"
Sewing machine, needle, thread

SORT THE COLORS:
Set aside the following
   5" x 5" squares to make
   half-square triangles:
   6 Red
   6 Olive
   6 Blue
   6 Blue Gray
   24 Cream/Light Prints

Set aside the remaining
   5" x 5" squares.
   Trim to 4 1/2" x 4 1/2":
   4 Light Green
   4 Goldish
      (3 Gold - 1 Green)
   20 Assorted
      (Green - Blue - Grey)

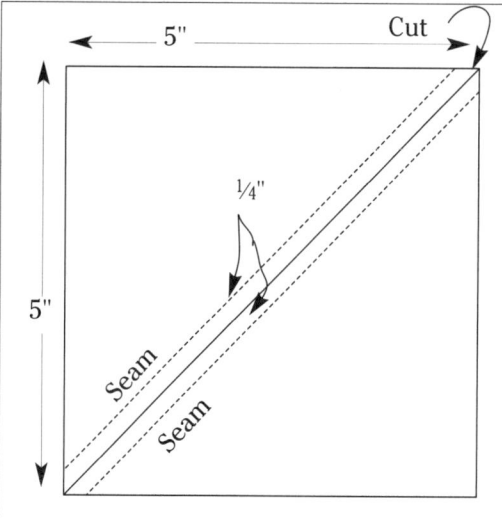

Half-Square Triangle Diagram
1. Place 2 squares right sides together.
2. Draw a diagonal line from corner to corner.
3. Stitch 1/4" on each side of the line.
4. Cut squares apart on the diagonal line.
5. Open the 2 new squares with 2 colors.
6. Press. Trim off dog-ears.
7. Trim to 4 1/2" x 4 1/2".

SEW HALF-SQUARE TRIANGLES:
Match the following squares for the half-square triangles:
   A - 6 pairs of Red - Cream/Light prints
   B - 6 pairs of Olive - Cream/Light prints
   C - 6 pairs of Blue - Cream/Light prints
   D - 6 pairs of Blue Gray - Cream/Light prints
Follow the instructions in the Half-Square Triangle
   Diagram to make all 48 half-square triangles.

SEW BLOCKS:
Arrange the 24 half-square triangles into pinwheel blocks
   and sew together.
   Press after each seam.

SEW THE CENTER:
Sew pinwheel blocks together following the diagram to
   make the quilt center.

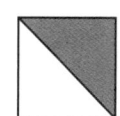

Half-Square Triangle
Use 24

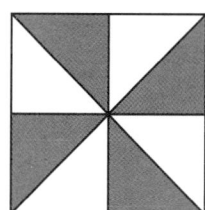

Pinwheel Block
(Sew 4 Half-Square
Triangles together)
Make 6 Blocks
(2 Red, 2 Olive, 2 Blue)

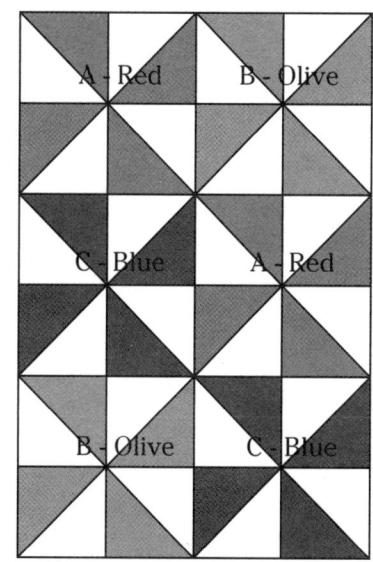

Quilt Center

SEW THE CORNER SECTIONS:
Arrange the 4-Patch squares as shown in the diagram.
   TIP: Make 3 with a Gold square and 1 with a Green square.
Sew 2 rows, 2 blocks per row to make a Corner Block.
   Press. Make 4.

 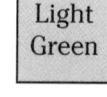

Corner Block Pieces

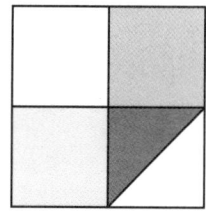

Corner Section
Make 4

SEW THE SIDE SECTIONS:

Following the diagram, sew
   6 half-square triangles
   into a column.

Sew 6 Assorted (Green -
   Blue - Gray) solid
   blocks into
   a column.

Press after each seam.
Sew the columns
   together as shown.

Make 2.

continued on page 12

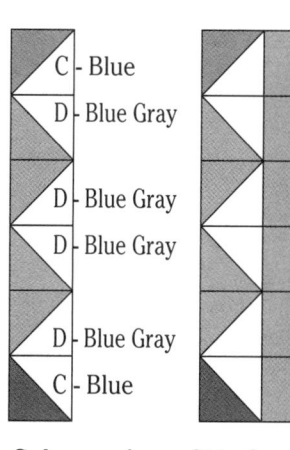

Column of   Side Section
Side Blocks   Make 2

Simply Strips & Squares 11

Kashmir - continued from pages 10 - 11

SEW TOP AND BOTTOM SECTIONS:
Following the diagram, sew 4 half-square triangles into a row.

Sew 4 Assorted (Green - Blue - Gray) solid blocks into a row.
Press after each seam.
Sew the rows together as shown.

Make 2.

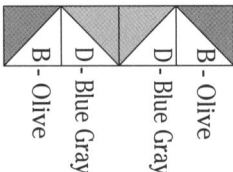

Row of Top & Bottom Blocks

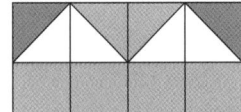

Top & Bottom Sections - Make 2

ASSEMBLE THE QUILT:
    Sew the Top and Bottom Sections to the Center Section.
        Press.
    Sew a Corner Section to the top and bottom of each Side Section.
        Press.
    Sew Side Sections to the Center Section.
        Press.

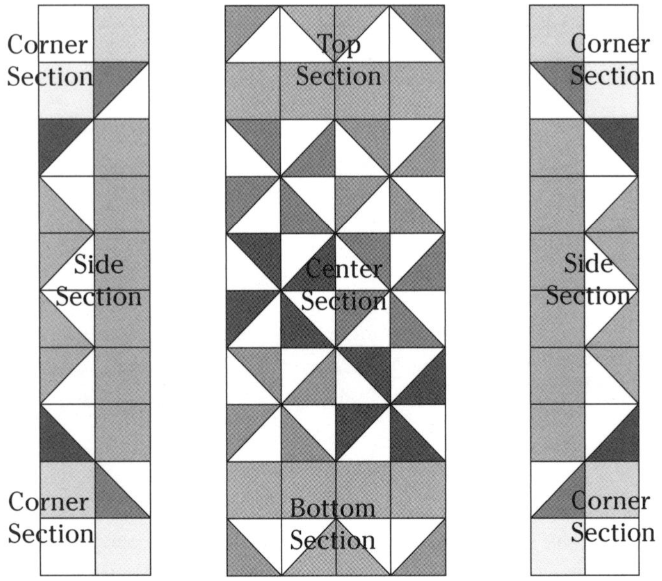

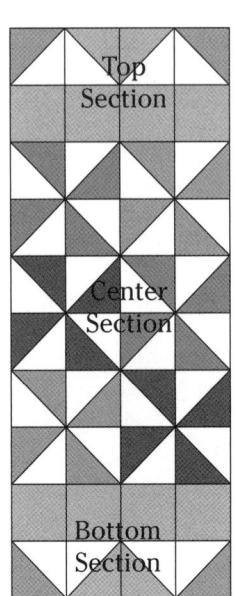

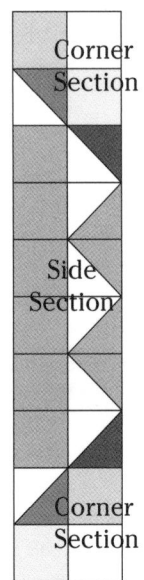

ADD THE BORDERS;
Inner Border #1:
Cut 4 strips 2½" wide.
Sew strips together end to end.
    Cut 2 strips 2½" x 40½" for sides.
    Cut 2 strips 2½" x 36½" for top and bottom.
    Sew side borders to the quilt. Press.
    Sew top and bottom borders to the quilt. Press.

Outer Border #2:
Cut 5 strips 4½" wide.
Sew strips together end to end.
    Cut 2 strips 4½" x 44½" for sides.
    Cut 2 strips 4½" x 44½" for top and bottom.
    Sew side borders to the quilt. Press.
    Sew top and bottom borders to the quilt. Press.

FINISHING:
Quilting:
    See Basic Instructions on pages 26 - 28.
Binding:
    Cut five 2½" strips.
    Sew together end to end to equal 200".
    See Binding Instructions on page 29.

Simply Strips & Squares

Daydreams Strips
photo on pages 4 - 5

SIZE: 60" x 68"

YARDAGE:
We used a *Moda* "Daydreams" by Deb Strain
  'Jelly Roll' collection of 2½" fabric strips
  - we purchased 1 'Jelly Roll'
  ½ yard Pink   OR   7 strips
  ½ yard Brown   OR   7 strips
  ⅔ yard Green   OR   9 strips
  ½ yard Aqua   OR   7 strips
  ¼ yard Ivory   OR   3 strips

Border #1   Purchase ½ yard Ivory
Border #2   Purchase ¼ yard Brown
Border #3 & Binding Purchase 1½ yards Pink
Backing   Purchase 3½ yards
Batting   Purchase 68" x 76"
Sewing machine, needle, thread

PREPARATION FOR BLOCKS
Organize your fabric strips.
Caution: Cut carefully. Cut the longest strips first.

BLOCK DIAGRAM:
Numbers indicate position and sewing sequence.

Cut the Lengths for Strips:
All cut strips are 2½" wide by the measurement given.
TIP: You may need to sew shorter strips of the same color,
  end to end, to enable you to cut a longer piece.
This just adds to the charm of the scrappy look.

Color   Quantity-Length
Blocks A & B -
Brown   8-10½"   8-8½"   8-6½"   8-4½"   8-2½"
Pink   8-8½"   8-6½"   8-4½"   8-2½"
  OPTIONAL: For center Blocks A & B, use Brown with Blue print.
  For outer Blocks A & B, use Brown with Pink print.

Block C & D -
Green   8-10½" 8-8½"   8-6½"   8-4½"   8-2½"
Aqua   8-10½" 8-8½"   8-6½"   8-4½"   8-2½"

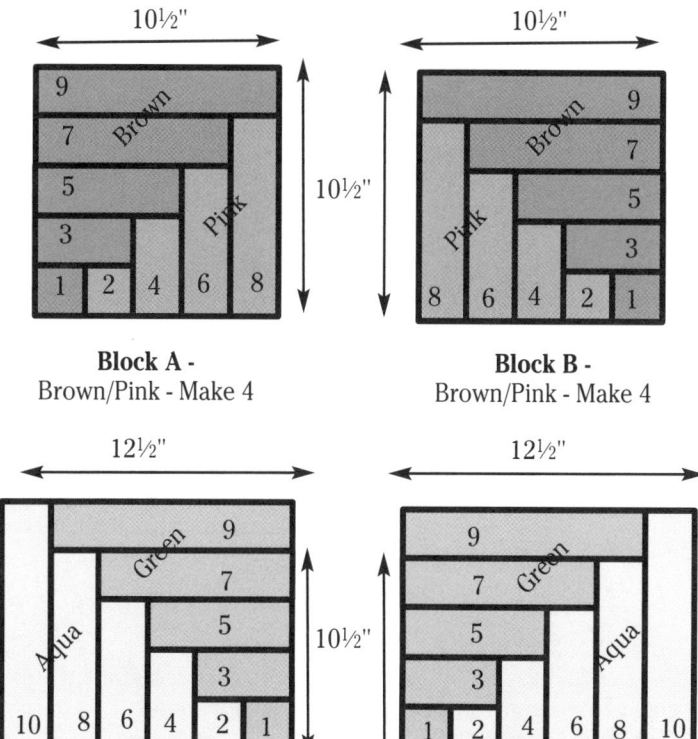

Block A - Brown/Pink - Make 4
Block B - Brown/Pink - Make 4
Block C - Green/Aqua - Make 4
Block D - Green/Aqua - Make 4

Sew the Following Color Blocks:
  Block A - Brown/Pink   make 4
  Block B - Brown/Pink   make 4
  Block C - Green/Aqua   make 4
  Block D - Green/Aqua   make 4

SEW BLOCKS:
Arrange strips according to block diagrams.
  Sew pieces together in numbered sequence.
  Press after each strip is sewn.

Sew 1 to 2, then add 3, then 4, 5, 6, etc. until block is complete.
  Blocks A & B will measure 10½" x 10½".
  Blocks C & D will measure 10½" x 12½".
  Label each block.

ASSEMBLY:
Center Section:
Arrange 2 Block As and 2 Block Bs on a work
  surface or table.
Refer to diagram for block placement and
  direction.
Sew blocks together in 2 rows, 2 blocks per row.
  Press.
Sew rows together. Press.

Center Border:
Use Ivory strips.
Cut 2 strips 2½" x 20½" for top and bottom.
Cut 2 strips 2½" x 24½" for sides.
Sew top and bottom borders to the quilt.
  Press.
Sew side borders to the quilt. Press.

continued on page 14

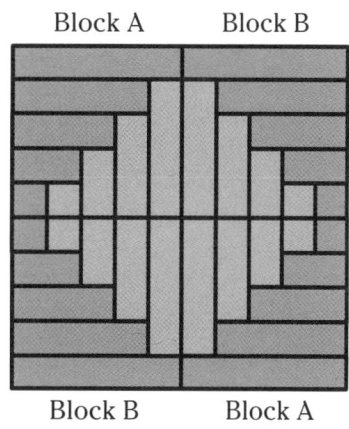

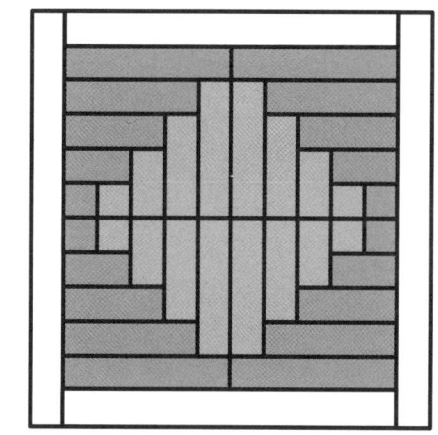

Center Section with Border

Daydreams Strips - continued from page 13

Side Columns:
Arrange Blocks C and D for the sides of the center piece.
Refer to diagram for block placement and direction.
Sew blocks together in 2 columns, 2 blocks per column. Press.
Make 2.

Center Row:
Sew the sections together. Press.

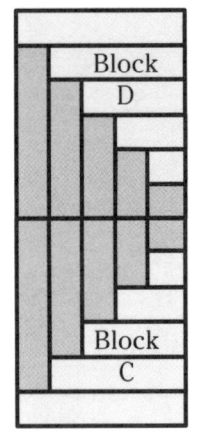
Side Columns - Make 2

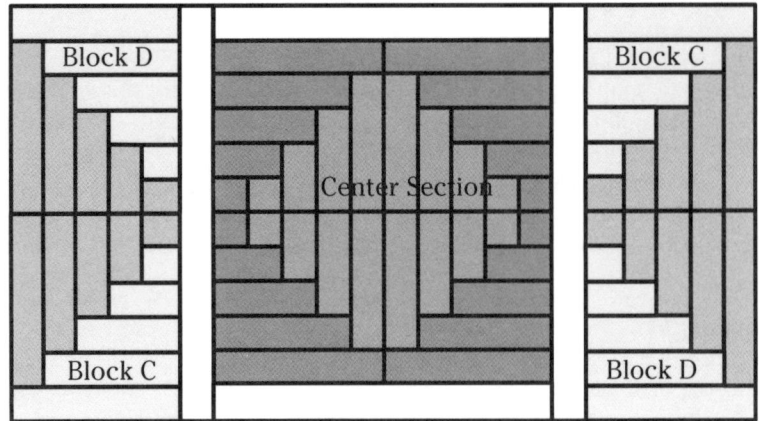
Center Row

Rows 1 & 3:
Arrange Blocks B, C, D and A on a table or work surface.
Refer to diagram for block placement and direction.
Sew blocks together.
Press.
Make 2.

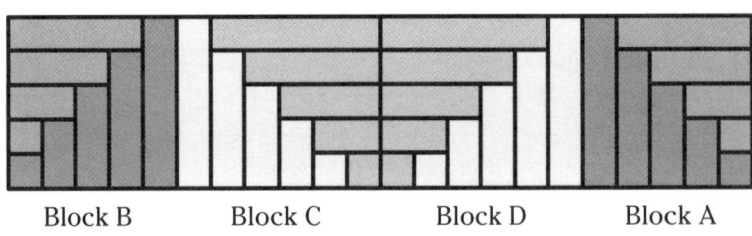
Rows 1 & 3 - Make 2

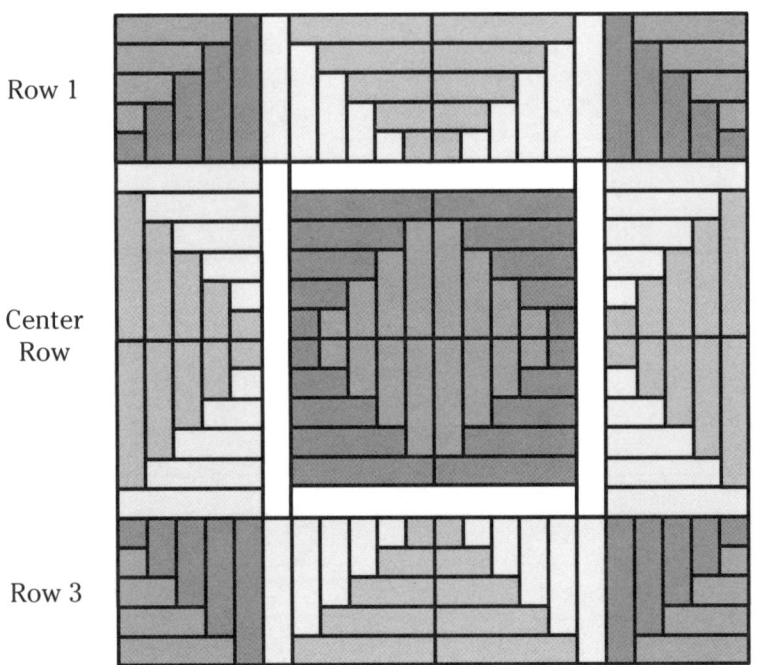

Assembly:
Sew rows 1 & 3 to the quilt center. Press.

Preparation to Make a Checkerboard:
Cut 2 Pink (P) strips 2½" x 30" long. Sew together side by side to make a piece 4½" x 30". Press.
Cut 2 Brown (B) strips 2½" x 20" long. Sew together side by side to make a piece 4½" x 20". Press.
Cut sewn strips into sections 2½" x 4½".

Top and Bottom Borders:
Cut the following Green strips: eight 10½", four 4½".
Arrange pieces as shown in the diagram.
Sew pieces together. Press. Make 2.

Sew 1 strip to the top and 1 strip to the bottom of the Center Section of the quilt. Press.
The Center Section is finished.

Top and Bottom Borders - Make 2

14 Simply Strips & Squares

Inner Border #1:
Cut 2½" strips.
Sew strips together end to end.
    Cut 2 strips 2½" x 52½" for sides.
    Cut 2 strips 2½" x 48½" for top and bottom.
    Sew side borders to the quilt. Press.
    Sew top and bottom borders to the quilt. Press.

Inner Border #2:
Cut 1½" strips.
Sew strips together end to end.
    Cut 2 strips 1½" x 56½" for sides.
    Cut 2 strips 1½" x 50½" for top and bottom.
    Sew side borders to the quilt. Press.
    Sew top and bottom borders to the quilt. Press

Outer Border #3:
Cut 5½" strips.
Sew strips together end to end.
    Cut 2 strips 5½" x 58½" for sides.
    Cut 2 strips 5½" x 60½" for top and bottom.
    Sew side borders to the quilt. Press.
    Sew top and bottom borders to the quilt. Press.

FINISHING:
Quilting: See Basic Instructions on pages 26 - 28.
Binding: Cut seven 2½" strips.
    Sew together end to end to equal 264".
    See Binding Instructions on page 29.

Daydreams Squares

photo is on page 4

SIZE: 38" x 42"

YARDAGE:
We used *Moda* "Daydreams" by Deb Strain
- we purchased 1 Charm Pack
(You'll need a total of 42 squares 5" x 5")
- 10 Brown OR ⅓ yard
- 5 White** OR ⅙ yard
- 9 Pink OR ⅓ yard
- 9 Aqua OR ⅓ yard
- 9 Green OR ⅓ yard

Border #1
 Purchase 1⅓ yards Pink border print
Binding Purchase ⅓ yard Pink print
Backing Purchase 1⅝ yards
Batting Purchase 46" x 50"
Sewing machine, needle, thread

**TIP: Use extra border or binding fabric to cut 2 White squares

SORT THE COLORS:
Set aside the following 5" x 5" squares and trim to 4½" x 4½":
- 1 White for Center row
- 2 Pink for Center row

Set aside the following 5" x 5" squares. Trim to 2½" x 4½":
- 1 Pink for Center row
- 9 Aqua for Pieced Border
- 9 Green for Pieced Border

Set aside the following 5" x 5" squares to make half-square triangles:
- 4 White
- 10 Brown
- 6 Pink

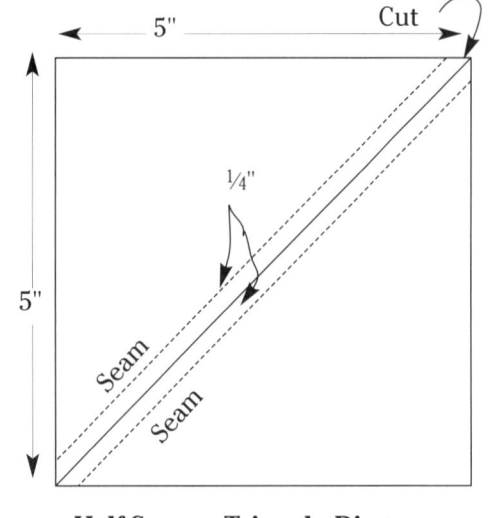

Half-Square Triangle Diagram
1. Place 2 squares right sides together.
2. Draw a diagonal line from corner to corner.
3. Stitch ¼" on each side of the line.
4. Cut squares apart on the diagonal line.
5. Open the 2 new squares with 2 colors.
6. Press. Trim off dog-ears.
7. Trim to 4½" x 4½".

SEW HALF SQUARE TRIANGLES:
Match the following squares for the half-square triangles:
- 4 pairs of White-Brown
- 6 pairs of Brown-Pink
Follow the instructions in the Half-Square Triangle Diagram to make all 20 half-square triangles.
Trim to 4½" x 4½".

 A. White-Brown
Make 8 (save 4 for later)

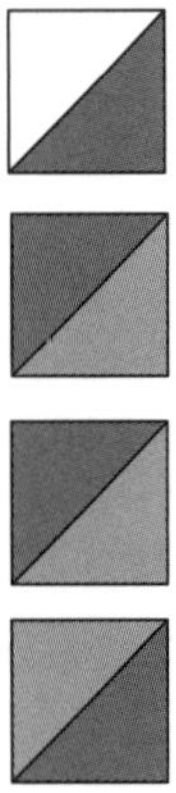

 B. Brown-Pink
Make 4

 C. Brown-Pink
Make 4

 D. Pink-Brown
Make 4

Half-Square Triangles for the 4-Patch Blocks

SEW 4-PATCH BLOCKS:
Arrange the half-square triangles into four 4-Patch blocks as shown.
Sew half-square triangles together for each row. Press.
Sew the rows together. Press.

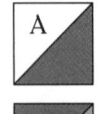 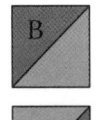

4-Patch for Diamond Section
Make 4

SEW DIAMOND SECTIONS:
Arrange the 4-Patch blocks as shown.
Sew 2 blocks together for each section. Press.

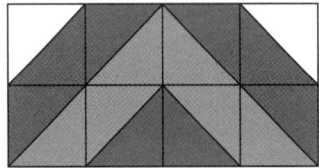

Diamond Section - Make 2

SEW CENTER ROW:
Line up
 a Pink square,
 a Pink 2½" x 4½" rectangle,
 a White square,
 a Pink 2½" x 4½" rectangle and
 a Pink square as shown.
Sew blocks together. Press.

Center Row - Make 1

PIECED BORDER PREPARATION:
Sew 1 Green 2½" x 4½" rectangle to an Aqua rectangle. Make 18 units. Press.

SIDE BORDER SECTIONS:
Using 5 Green-Aqua Border units, sew a column of 5 units. Press. Make 2.

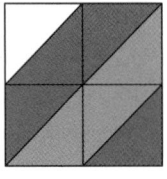

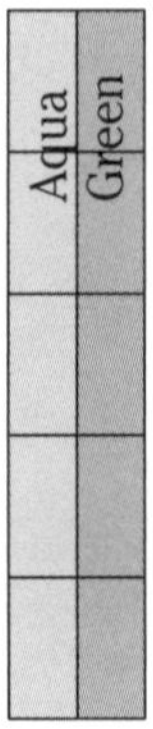

Side Border Section - Make 2

SEW TOP & BOTTOM BORDER SECTIONS:
Sew 4 Green-Aqua Border units in a row. Press.
Sew a White-Brown Corner block to each end. Press.
Make 2.

 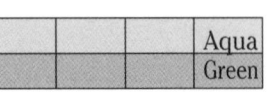

White/Brown Corner Block Green and Aqua Border Make 2

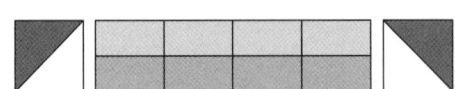

Top & Bottom Border Assembly - Make 2

16 *Simply Strips & Squares*

ASSEMBLE THE QUILT:
- Sew the Center sections together. Press.
- Sew Side sections to the Quilt Center. Press.
- Sew the Top and Bottom sections to the Quilt Center. Press.

Section Assembly

ADD THE BORDERS;
Mitered Border:
  Cut 2 strips 7½" x 44" for the sides.
  Cut 2 strips 7½" x 40" for the top and bottom.
Follow the instructions for Mitered Borders.

FINISHING:
Quilting: See Basic Instructions on pages 26 - 28.
Binding: Cut four 2½" strips.
  Sew together end to end to equal 168".
  See Binding Instructions on page 29.

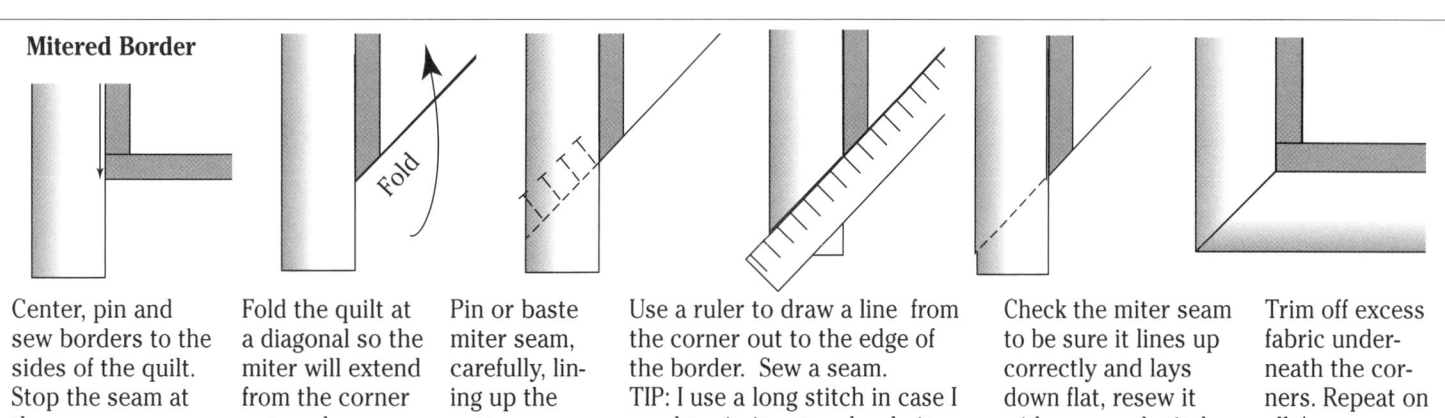

Simply Strips & Squares

A Morris Garden Squares

photo is on page 6

SIZE: 26" x 34"

YARDAGE:
We used Moda "A Morris Garden" by Barbara Brackman
- we purchased 1 Charm Pack
 (You'll need a total of 24 squares 5" x 5")
 1 Brown   OR   ⅙ yard
 2 Gold   OR   ⅙ yard
 1 Navy/Black   OR   ⅙ yard
 2 Medium Blue   OR   ⅙ yard
 4 Light Blue   OR   ⅙ yard
 6 Black prints   OR   ⅙ yard
 8 Tan/Lt Green prints OR ⅓ yard

Border #1 & Binding   Purchase ½ yard Medium Blue
Border #2   Purchase ⅜ yard Light Blue
Backing   Purchase 1⅙ yards
Batting   Purchase 34" x 42"
Sewing machine, needle, thread

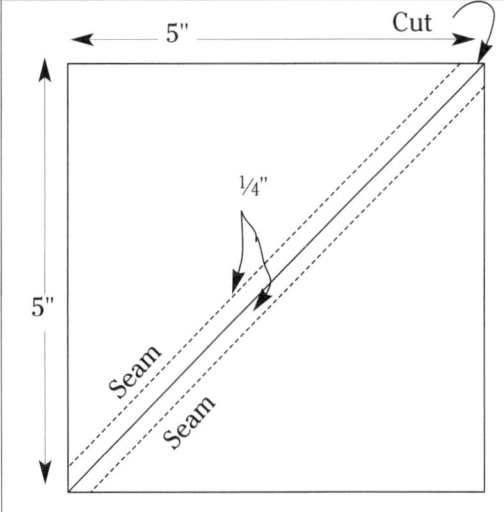

Half-Square Triangle Diagram
1. Place 2 squares right sides together.
2. Draw a diagonal line from corner to corner.
3. Stitch ¼" on each side of the line.
4. Cut squares apart on the diagonal line.
5. Open the 2 new squares with 2 colors.
6. Press. Trim off dog-ears.
7. Trim to 4½" x 4½".

SORT THE COLORS:
Set aside the following 5" x 5" squares and trim to 4½" x 4½".
 8 Tan/Light Green prints

Set aside the following 5" x 5" squares to make half-square triangles:
 1 Brown
 2 Gold
 1 Navy/Black
 2 Medium Blue
 4 Light Blue
 6 Black prints

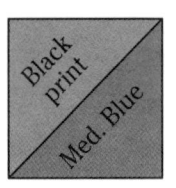
Make 4

Make 4

HALF-SQUARE TRIANGLES:
Match the following squares for the half-square triangles:
 2 pair of Black print - Medium Blue
 4 pair of Black print - Light Blue
 2 pair of Navy/Black or Brown - Gold

Follow the instructions in the Half-Square Triangle Diagram
 to make all 16 half-square triangles.
Trim to 4½" x 4½".

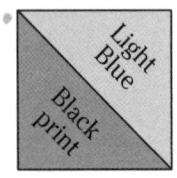
Make 4

Make 4

Half-Square Triangles

SEW BLOCKS:
Arrange the half-square triangles into four 4-Patch blocks as shown.
Sew half-square triangles together for each row. Press.
Sew the rows together. Press.

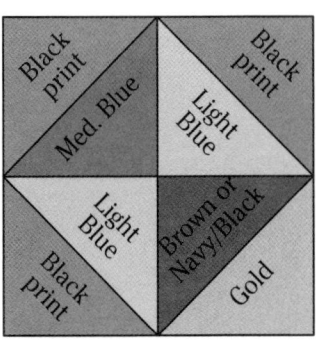

4-Patch Block
Make 4

18 Simply Strips & Squares

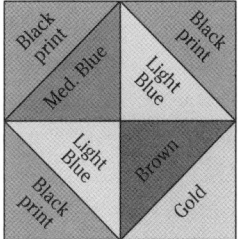 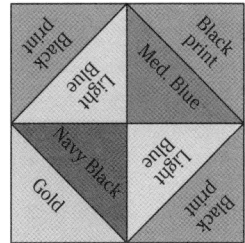

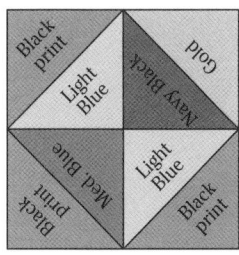 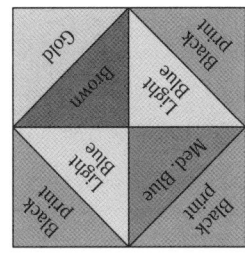

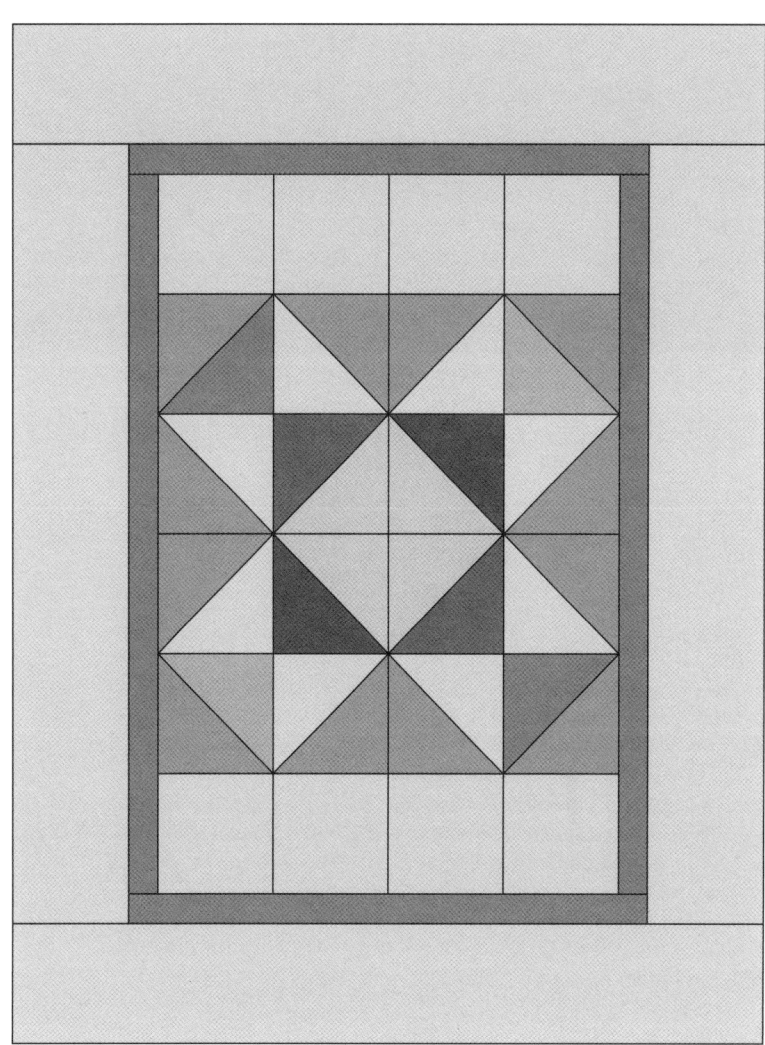

CENTER SECTION ASSEMBLY:
  Arrange the 4-Patch Blocks on a work surface or table.
  Refer to diagram for block placement and direction.
  Sew blocks together in 2 rows, 2 blocks per row. Press.
  Sew rows together. Press.

Center Section

TOP AND BOTTOM ROW ASSEMBLY:
  Sew 4 Tan/Lt. Green print blocks together to form a row. Make 2.
  Press.
  Sew a row to the top and to the bottom of the Center Section.
  Press.

ADD the borders:
Inner Border #1:
  Cut 2 strips 1½" x 24½" for sides.
  Cut 2 strips 1½" x 18½" for top and bottom.
  Sew side borders to the quilt. Press.
  Sew top and bottom borders to the quilt. Press.

Outer Border #2:
  Cut 2 strips 4½" x 26½" for sides.
  Cut 2 strips 4½" x 26½" for top and bottom.
  Sew side borders to the quilt. Press.
  Sew top and bottom borders to the quilt. Press.

FINISHING:
Quilting: See Basic Instructions on pages 26 - 28.
Binding: Cut four 2½" strips.
  Sew together end to end to equal 130".
  See Binding Instructions on page 29.

Top & Bottom Row

Simply Strips & Squares 19

A Morris Garden Strips Log Cabin Window Blocks

photo is on pages 6 - 7

SIZE: 48" x 58"

YARDAGE:
We used a Moda "A Morris Garden" by Barbara Brackman
  'Jelly Roll' collection of 2½" fabric strips
  - we purchased 1 'Jelly Roll'
  ⅓ yard Gold   OR   4 strips
  ⅓ yard Dark Blue   OR   4 strips
  ½ yard Light Blue   OR   6 strips
  ⅝ yard Black print   OR   8 strips
  ⅔ yard Greenish   OR   9 strips
Border & Binding   Purchase 1½ yard Black print
Backing   Purchase 2⅞ yards
Batting   Purchase 56" x 66"
Sewing machine, needle, thread

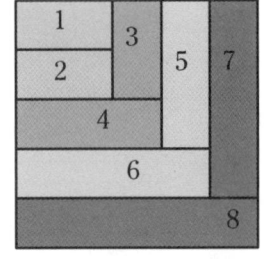

Modified Log Cabin Block
Make 12

PREPARATION FOR BLOCKS
  #1 and #2 - Cut 24 Gold strips 2½" x 4½".
  #3 - Cut 12 Darkest Blue strips 2½" x 4½".
  #4 - Cut 12 Dark Blue strips 2½" x 6½".
  #5 - Cut 12 Lightest Blue strips 2½" x 6½".
  #6 - Cut 12 Light Blue strips 2½" x 8½".
  #7 - Cut 12 Black print strips 2½" x 8½".
  #8 - Cut 12 Black print strips 2½" x 10½".

SEW THE BLOCKS:
  See the Modified Log Cabin Block for placement.
  For each block, sew #1 to #2. Press.
  Sew #3 to the right side of the block. Press.
  Sew #4 to the bottom of the block. Press.
  Sew #5 to the right side of the block. Press.
  Sew #6 to the bottom of the block. Press.
  Sew #7 to the right side of the block. Press.
  Sew #8 to the bottom of the block. Press.
  Each block will measure 10½" x 10½" at this point.

ASSEMBLE THE BLOCKS:
  Arrange all Blocks on a work surface or table.
  Refer to diagram for block placement and direction.
  Sew blocks together in 4 rows, 3 blocks per row. Press.
  Sew rows together. Press.

SEW THE FRAMES:
  Cut 3 Black strips 2½" x 10½" for Top Frame.
  Sew strips together end to end. Press.
  For Left Frame, cut 1 Black strip 2½" x 12½" and
    3 Black strips 2½" x 10½".
  Sew strips together end to end, beginning with the
    12½" strip at the top. Press.

ADD THE FRAME STRIPS:
  Sew Top Frame to the block assembly. Press.
  Sew Left Frame to the block assembly. Press.

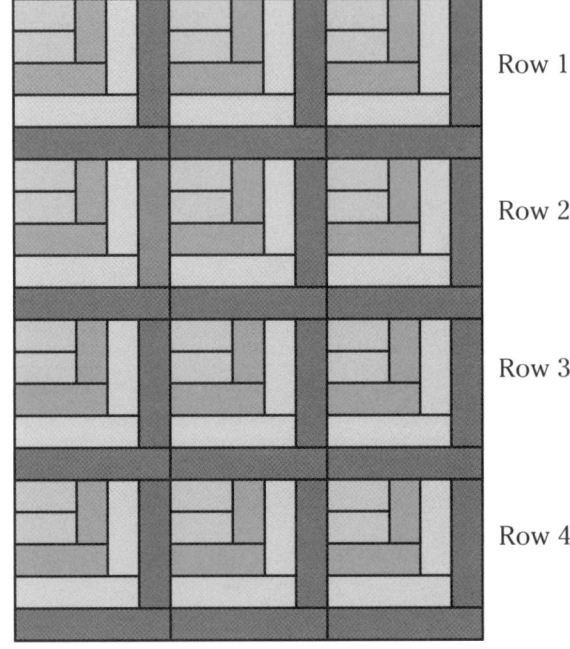

Block Assembly Diagram (Row 1, Row 2, Row 3, Row 4)

Top Black Frame - Make 1

Left Side Black Frame Make 1

Finished Quilt Center

20 Simply Strips & Squares

ADD THE BORDERS:
Pieced Border #1:
Sew 4 leftover Greenish strips together end to end.
    Cut 2 strips 2½" x 42½" for sides.
    Cut 2 strips 2½" x 36½" for top and bottom.
    Sew side borders to the quilt. Press.
    Sew top and bottom borders to the quilt. Press.

Pieced Border #2:
Sew 5 leftover Greenish strips together end to end.
    Cut 2 strips 2½" x 46½" for sides.
    Cut 2 strips 2½" x 40½" for top and bottom.
    Sew side borders to the quilt. Press.
    Sew top and bottom borders to the quilt. Press.

Outer Border #3:
Cut 4½" strips.
Sew strips together end to end.
    Cut 2 strips 4½" x 50½" for sides.
    Cut 2 strips 4½" x 48½" for top and bottom.
    Sew side borders to the quilt. Press.
    Sew top and bottom borders to the quilt. Press.

FINISHING:
Quilting: See Basic Instructions on pages 26 - 28.
Binding: Cut six 2½" strips.
    Sew together end to end to equal 220".
    See Binding Instructions on page 29.

Red, White, and Bold Squares Charms Quilt

photo is on page 8

SIZE: 28" x 36"

YARDAGE:
We used Moda "Red, White, & Bold" by Sandy Gervais
- we purchased 1 Charm Pack
(You'll need a total of 35 squares 5" x 5")

12 Ivory print	OR	⅓ yard
6 Red print	OR	⅙ yard
6 Navy print	OR	⅙ yard
11 Blue print	OR	⅓ yard

Border #2 & Binding — Purchase ⅞ yard Dark Blue
Backing — Purchase 1¼ yards
Batting — Purchase 36" x 44"
Sewing machine, needle, thread

SORT THE COLORS:
Set aside 11 Blue 5" x 5" squares for the Pieced Border #1.
Set aside the following 5" x 5" squares to make half-square triangles:
 6 Red
 6 Navy
 12 Ivory

HALF-SQUARE TRIANGLES:
Match the following squares for the half-square triangles:
 6 pairs of Red-Ivory
 6 pairs of Navy-Ivory
Follow the instructions in the Half-Square Triangle Diagram to make all 24 half-square triangles.
Trim to 4½" x 4½".

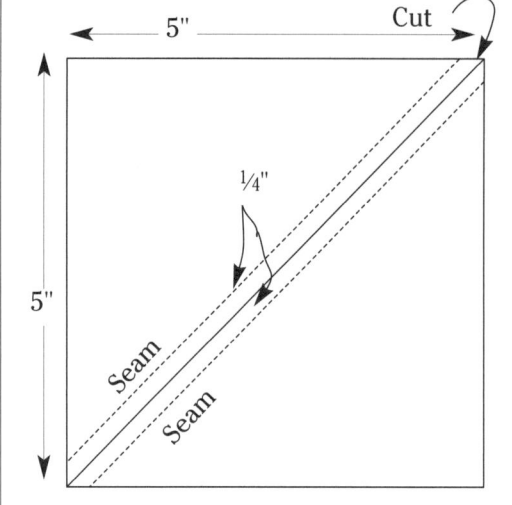

Half-Square Triangle Diagram
1. Place 2 squares right sides together.
2. Draw a diagonal line from corner to corner.
3. Stitch ¼" on each side of the line.
4. Cut squares apart on the diagonal line.
5. Open the 2 new squares with 2 colors.
6. Press. Trim off dog-ears.
7. Trim to 4½" x 4½".

SEW THE BLOCKS:
Arrange the Navy half-square triangles into a Pinwheel block.
Arrange the Red half-square triangles into an Hourglass block.
Sew half-square triangles together.
 Press.
Make 3 of each block.

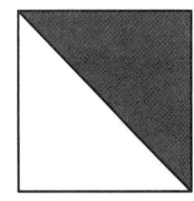 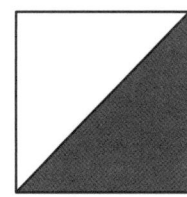

Navy-Ivory Half-Square Triangles - Make 3 sets (12 of each)

 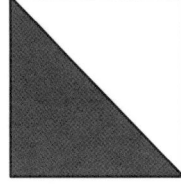

Navy-Ivory Pinwheel Block
Make 3

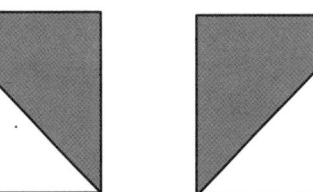

Red-Ivory Half-Square Triangles - Make 3 sets (12 of each)

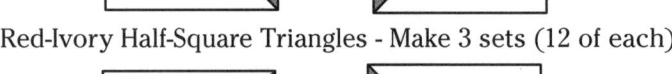

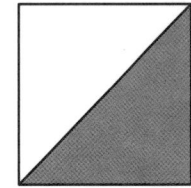 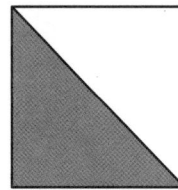

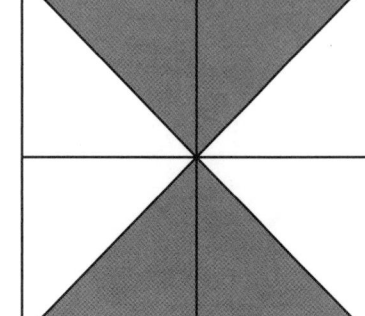

Red-Ivory Hourglass Block
Make 3

ASSEMBLY:
  Arrange all Blocks on a work surface or table.
  Refer to diagram for block placement and direction.
  Sew blocks together in 3 rows, 2 blocks per row. Press.
  Sew rows together. Press.

ADD THE BORDERS:
Pieced Inner Border #1:
Corners:
  Cut 1 Blue print square in half twice to make 4 squares 2½" x 2½".
Sides:
  Cut 6 Blue print squares in half to make 12 rectangles 2½" x 5".
  Sew all strips together end to end.
  Center and cut 2 strips 2½" x 24½".
Top & Bottom:
  Cut 4 Blue print squares in half to make 8 rectangles 2½" x 5".
  Trim each to 2½" x 4½".
  Sew 4 strips together end to end for the top border.
  Sew a Corner square to each end of the strip.
  Repeat for the bottom border.

Sew side borders to the quilt. Press.
Sew top and bottom borders to the quilt. Press.

Outer Border #2:
  Cut 2 strips 4½" x 28½" for sides.
  Cut 2 strips 4½" x 28½" for top and bottom.
  Sew side borders to the quilt. Press.
  Sew top and bottom borders to the quilt. Press.

FINISHING:
Quilting: See Basic Instructions on pages 26 - 28.
Binding: Cut four 2½" strips.
  Sew together end to end to equal 138".
  See Binding Instructions on page 29.

Red, White & Bold Strips
Squares in Squares

photo is on pages 8 - 9

SIZE: 52" x 66"

YARDAGE:
We used *Moda* "Red, White, & Bold" by Sandy Gervais
  'Jelly Roll' collection of 2½" fabric strips
  - we purchased 1 'Jelly Roll'
  ⅙ yard Red print   OR   3 strips
  ⅝ yard Navy print   OR   9 strips
  ¾ yard White print   OR   11 strips
  ⅔ yard Blue print   OR   9 strips
Border #1   Purchase ¼ yard Red
Border #2 & Binding   Purchase 1⅛ yards Navy
Backing   Purchase 3⅛ yards
Batting   Purchase 60" x 74"
Sewing machine, needle, thread

FOR BLOCK A, to make 3:
#1, 2, & 3 - Cut 9 Red strips 2½" x 6½".
#4 & 5 - Cut 6 Navy strips 2½" x 6½".
#6 & 7 - Cut 6 Navy strips 2½" x 10½".
#8 & 9 - Cut 6 White strips 2½" x 10½".
#10 & 11 - Cut 6 White strips 2½" x 14½".

FOR BLOCK B, to make 3:
#1, 2, & 3 - Cut 9 White strips 2½" x 6½".
#4 & 5 - Cut 6 Navy strips 2½" x 6½".
#6 & 7 - Cut 6 Navy strips 2½" x 10½".
#8 & 9 - Cut 6 Blue strips 2½" x 10½".
#10 & 11 - Cut 6 Blue strips 2½" x 14½".

FOR BLOCK C, to make 3:
#1, 2, & 3 - Cut 9 Red strips 2½" x 6½".
#4 & 5 - Cut 6 Blue strips 2½" x 6½".
#6 & 7 - Cut 6 Blue strips 2½" x 10½".
#8 & 9 - Cut 6 White strips 2½" x 10½".
#10 & 11 - Cut 6 White strips 2½" x 14½".

FOR BLOCK D, to make 3:
#1, 2, & 3 - Cut 9 White strips 2½" x 6½".
#4 & 5 - Cut 6 Blue strips 2½" x 6½".
#6 & 7 - Cut 6 Blue strips 2½" x 10½".
#8 & 9 - Cut 6 Navy strips 2½" x 10½".
#10 & 11 - Cut 6 Navy strips 2½" x 14½".

SEW BLOCKS A, B, C, AND D:
Sew 3 center strips 1-2-3 together. Press.
Sew strips 4 and 5 to 1-2-3. Press.
Sew strips 6 and 7 to the block. Press.
Sew strips 8 and 9 to the block. Press.
Sew strips 10 and 11 to the block. Press.
Each block will measure 14½" x 14½" at this point.

ASSEMBLE THE QUILT:
Arrange all Blocks on a work surface or table.
Refer to diagram for block placement and direction.
Sew blocks together in 4 rows, 3 blocks per row.
  Press.
Sew rows together. Press.

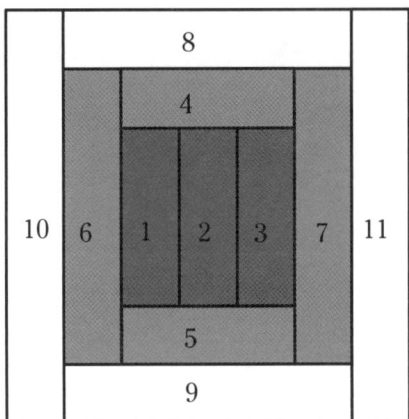

Block A - Make 3

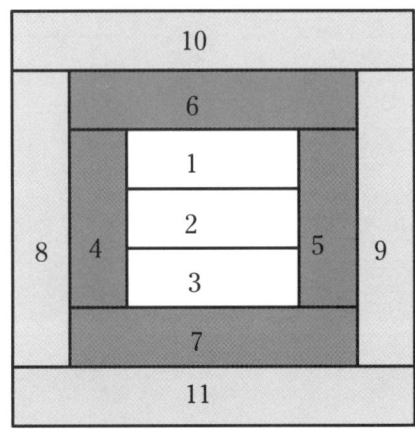

Block B - Make 3

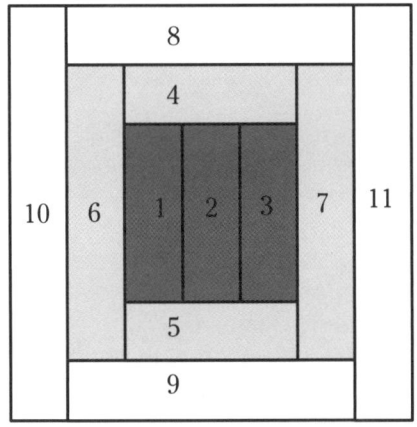

Block C - Make 3

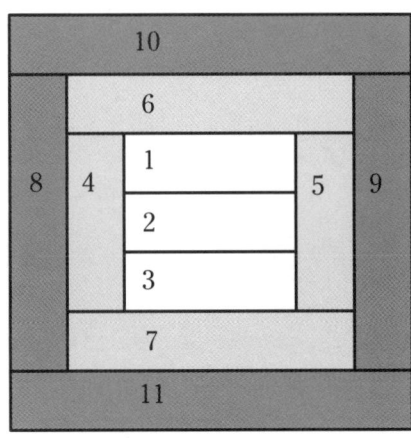

Block D - Make 3

24   Simply Strips & Squares

ADD THE BORDERS:
Border #1:
Cut 1½" strips.
Sew strips together end to end.
    Cut 2 strips 1½" x 56½" for sides.
    Cut 2 strips 1½" x 44½" for top and bottom.
    Sew side borders to the quilt. Press.
    Sew top and bottom borders to the quilt. Press.

Border #2:
Cut 4½" strips.
Sew strips together end to end.
    Cut 2 strips 4½" x 58½" for sides.
    Cut 2 strips 4½" x 52½" for top and bottom.
    Sew side borders to the quilt. Press.
    Sew top and bottom borders to the quilt. Press.

FINISHING:
Quilting:
    See Basic Instructions on pages 26 - 28.
Binding:
    Cut six 2½" strips.
    Sew together end to end to equal 244".
    See Binding Instructions on page 29.

Simply Strips & Squares 25

The Best Things About Jelly Rolls

I love to quilt, but it is often difficult to find time to cut and piece a quilt top. When I saw the 'Jelly Roll' collections of 2½" pre-cut fabric strips, I knew they were the answer.

No more spending hours choosing and cutting fabrics. Now I can begin sewing right away. Beautiful colors are available in every 'Jelly Roll'. So whether I like jewel colors, heritage patterns, soft pastels or earthy tones... there is an assortment for me.

Now my goals... a handmade cover for every bed, an heirloom quilt for each new baby and a pieced quilt for each of my children is in reach. With 'Jelly Rolls' it is possible to complete a quilt top in a weekend.

After I piece all the blocks together, I use leftover strips for the borders and binding. Nothing really goes to waste and, if needed, I can purchase a bit of extra fabric for an extra punch of color or an additional yard for the border.

TIP: With the patterns in this book, the quantities are given so you know what color strips you need and can start right away.

Design Tips with 'Charm Squares'

I love quilting with 'Charm' collections of pre-cut 5" x 5" fabric pieces. I want to share a few tips for working with 'Charm Squares'. The colors are always beautiful together and create the handmade scrappy look that is so popular today.

My first step in designing is to divide the 5" squares into groups of color... Greens, Purples, Browns, Tans, etc. Next I estimate the number of squares I will need for the center of the quilt.

Sometimes I need an extra square or two of a color, let's say Dark Brown so I look for a Tan print with a lot of Brown and move it to the Dark Brown stack.... and the same with other colors.

Enjoy quilting..

Tips for Working with Strips

TIPS: As a Guide for Yardage:
Each ¼ yard or a 'Fat Quarter' equals 3 strips
A pre-cut 'Jelly Roll' strip is 2½" x 44"
Cut 'Fat Quarter' strips to 2½" x 22"

Pre-cut strips are cut on the crosswise grain and are prone to stretching. These tips will help reduce stretching and make your quilt lay flat for quilting.

1. If you are cutting yardage, cut on the grain. Cut fat quarters on grain, parallel to the 18" side.

2. When sewing crosswise grain strips together, take care not to stretch the strips. If you detect any puckering as you go, rip out the seam and sew it again.

3. Press, Do Not Iron. Carefully open fabric, with the seam to one side, press without moving the iron. A back-and-forth ironing motion stretches the fabric.

4. Reduce the wiggle in your borders with this technique from garment making. First, accurately cut your borders to the exact measure of the quilt top. Then, before sewing the border to the quilt, run a double row of stay stitches along the outside edge to maintain the original shape and prevent stretching. Pin the border to the quilt, taking care not to stretch the quilt top to make it fit. Pinning reduces slipping and stretching.

Rotary Cutting Tips

Rotary Cutter: Friend or Foe

A rotary cutter is wonderful and useful. When not used correctly, the sharp blade can be a dangerous tool. Follow these safety tips:

1. Never cut toward you.
2. Use a sharp blade. Pressing harder on a dull blade can cause the blade to jump the ruler and injure your fingers.
3. Always disengage the blade before the cutter leaves your hand, even if you intend to pick it up immediately.

Rotary cutters have been caught when lifting fabric, have fallen onto the floor and have cut fingers.

Basic Cutting Instructions

Tips for Accurate Cutting:

Accurate cutting is easy when using a rotary cutter with a sharp blade, a cutting mat, and a transparent ruler. Begin by pressing your fabric and then follow these steps:

1. Folding:

a) Fold the fabric with the selvage edges together. Smooth the fabric flat. If needed, fold again to make your fabric length smaller than the length of the ruler.

b) Align the fold with one of the guide lines on the mat. This is important to avoid getting a kink in your strip.

2. Cutting:

a) Align the ruler with a guide line on the mat. Press down on the ruler to prevent it shifting or have someone help hold the ruler. Hold the rotary cutter along the edge of the ruler and cut off the selvage edge.

b) Also using the guide line on the mat, cut the ends straight.

c) Strips for making the quilt top may be cut on 'crosswise grain' (from selvage to selvage) or 'on grain' (parallel to the selvage edge).

Strips for borders should be cut on grain (parallel to the selvage edge) to prevent wavy edges and make quilting easier.

d) When cutting strips, move the ruler, NOT the fabric.

Basic Sewing Instructions

You now have precisely cut strips that are exactly the correct width. You are well on your way to blocks that fit together perfectly. Accurate sewing is the next important step.

Matching Edges:

1. Carefully line up the edges of your strips. Many times, if the underside is off a little, your seam will be off by $1/8$". This does not sound like much until you have 8 seams in a block, each off by $1/8$". Now your finished block is a whole inch wrong!

2. Pin the pieces together to prevent them shifting.

Seam Allowance:

I cannot stress enough the importance of accurate $1/4$" seams. All the quilts in this book are measured for $1/4$" seams unless otherwise indicated.

Most sewing machine manufacturers offer a Quarter-inch foot. A Quarter-inch foot is the most worthwhile investment you can make in your quilting.

Pressing:

I want to talk about pressing even before we get to sewing because proper pressing can make the difference between a quilt that wins a ribbon at the quilt show and one that does not.

Press, do NOT iron. What does that mean? Many of us want to move the iron back and forth along the seam. This "ironing" stretches the strip out of shape and creates errors that accumulate as the quilt is constructed. Believe it or not, there is a correct way to press your seams, and here it is:

1. Do NOT use steam with your iron. If you need a little water, spritz it on.

2. Place your fabric flat on the ironing board without opening the seam. Set a hot iron on the seam and count to 3. Lift the iron and move to the next position along the seam. Repeat until the entire seam is pressed. This sets and sinks the threads into the fabric.

3. Now, carefully lift the top strip and fold it away from you so the seam is on one side. Usually the seam is pressed toward the darker fabric, but often the direction of the seam is determined by the piecing requirements.

4. Press the seam open with your fingers. Add a little water or spray starch if it wants to close again. Lift the iron and place it on the seam. Count to 3. Lift the iron again and continue until the seam is pressed. Do NOT use the tip of the iron to push the seam open. So many people do this and wonder later why their blocks are not fitting together.

5. Most critical of all: For accuracy every seam must be pressed before the next seam is sewn.

Working with 'Crosswise Grain' strips:

Strips cut on the crosswise grain (from selvage to selvage) have problems similar to bias edges and are prone to stretching. To reduce stretching and make your quilt lay flat for quilting, keep these tips in mind.

1. Take care not to stretch the strips as you sew.

2. Adjust the sewing thread tension and the presser foot pressure if needed.

3. If you detect any puckering as you go, rip out the seam and sew it again. It is much easier to take out a seam now than to do it after the block is sewn.

Sewing Bias Edges:

Bias edges wiggle and stretch out of shape very easily. They are not recommended for beginners, but even a novice can accomplish bias edges if these techniques are employed.

1. Stabilize the bias edge with one of these methods:

a) Press with spray starch.

b) Press freezer paper or removable iron-on stabilizer to the back of the fabric.

c) Sew a double row of stay stitches along the bias edge and $1/8$" from the bias edge. This is a favorite technique of garment makers.

2. Pin, pin, pin! I know many of us dislike pinning, but when working with bias edges, pinning makes the difference between intersections that match and those that do not.

Building Better Borders:

Wiggly borders make a quilt very difficult to finish. However, wiggly borders can be avoided with these techniques.

1. Cut the borders on grain. That means cutting your strips parallel to the selvage edge.

2. Accurately cut your borders to the exact measure of the quilt.

3. If your borders are piece stripped from crosswise grain fabrics, press well with spray starch and sew a double row of stay stitches along the outside edge to maintain the original shape and prevent stretching.

4. Pin the border to the quilt, taking care not to stretch the quilt top to make it fit. Pinning reduces slipping and stretching.

Applique Instructions

Basic Turned Edge

1. Trace pattern onto template plastic.

2. Cut out the shape leaving a scant ¼" fabric border all around and clip the curves.

3. Place the template plastic on the wrong side of the fabric. Spray edges with starch.

4. Press the ⅛" border over the edge of the template plastic with the tip of a hot iron. Press firmly.

5. Remove the template, maintaining the folded edge on the back of the fabric.

6. Position the shape on the quilt and Blindstitch in place.

Basic Needle Turn

1. Cut out the shape leaving a ¼" fabric border all around.

2. Baste the shapes to the quilt, keeping the basting stitches away from the edge of the fabric.

3. Begin with all areas that are under other layers and work to the topmost layer.

4. For an area no more than 2" ahead of where you are working, trim to ⅛" and clip the curves.

5. Using the needle, roll the edge under and sew tiny Blindstitches to secure.

Using Fusible Web for Iron-on Applique:

1. Trace the pattern onto *Steam a Seam 2* fusible web.

2. Press the patterns onto the wrong side of the fabric.

3. Cut out patterns exactly on the drawn line.

4. Score the web paper with a pin, then remove the paper.

5. Position the fabric, fusible side down, on the quilt. Press with a hot iron following the fusible web manufacturer's instructions.

6. Stitch around the edge by hand.

Optional: Stabilize the wrong side of the fabric with your favorite stabilizer.

Use a size 80 machine embroidery needle. Fill the bobbin with lightweight basting thread and thread the machine with a machine embroidery thread that complements the color being appliqued.

Set your machine for a Zigzag stitch and adjust the thread tension if needed. Use a scrap to experiment with different stitch widths and lengths until you find the one you like best.

Sew slowly.

Basic Layering Instructions

Marking Your Quilt:

If you choose to mark your quilt for hand or machine quilting, it is much easier to do so before layering. Press your quilt before you begin. Here are some handy tips regarding marking.

1. A disappearing pen may vanish before you finish.

2. Use a White pencil on dark fabrics.

3. If using a washable Blue pen, remember that pressing may make the pen permanent.

Pieced Backings:

1. Press the backing fabric before measuring.

2. If possible cut backing fabrics on grain, parallel to the selvage edges.

3. Piece 3 parts rather than 2 whenever possible, sewing 2 side borders to the center. This reduces stress on the pieced seam.

4. The backing and batting should extend at least 2" on each side of the quilt.

Creating a Quilt Sandwich:

1. Press the backing and top to remove all wrinkles.

2. Lay the backing wrong side up on the table.

3. Position the batting over the backing and smooth out all wrinkles.

4. Center the quilt top over the batting leaving a 2" border all around.

5. Pin the layers together with 2" safety pins positioned a handwidth apart. A grapefruit spoon makes inserting the pins easier. Leaving the pins open in the container speeds up the basting on the next quilt.

Basic Quilting Instructions

Hand Quilting:

Many quilters enjoy the serenity of hand quilting. Because the quilt is handled a great deal, it is important to securely baste the sandwich together. Place the quilt in a hoop and don't forget to hide your knots.

Machine Quilting:

All the quilts in this book were machine quilted. Some were quilted on a large, free-arm quilting machine and others were quilted on a sewing machine. If you have never machine quilted before, practice on some scraps first.

Straight Line Machine Quilting Tips:

1. Pin baste the layers securely.

2. Set up your sewing machine with a size 80 quilting needle and a walking foot.

3. Experimenting with the decorative stitches on your machine adds interest to your quilt. You do not have to quilt the entire piece with the same stitch. Variety is the spice of life, so have fun trying out stitches you have never used before as well as your favorite stand-bys.

Free Motion Machine Quilting Tips:

1. Pin baste the layers securely.

2. Set up your sewing machine with a spring needle, a quilting foot, and lower the feed dogs.

28 Simply Strips & Squares

Basic Mitered Binding Instructions

A Perfect Finish:

The binding endures the most stress on a quilt and is usually the first thing to wear out. For this reason, we recommend using a double fold binding.

1. Trim the backing and batting even with the quilt edge.

2. If possible cut strips on the crosswise grain because a little bias in the binding is a Good thing. This is the only place in the quilt where bias is helpful, for it allows the binding to give as it is turned to the back and sewn in place.

3. Strips are usually cut 2½" wide, but check the instructions for your project before cutting.

4. Sew strips end to end to make a long strip sufficient to go all around the quilt plus 4"- 6".

5. With wrong sides together, fold the strip in half lengthwise. Press.

6. Stretch out your hand and place your little finger at the corner of the quilt top. Place the binding where your thumb touches the edge of the quilt. Aligning the edge of the quilt with the raw edges of the binding, pin the binding in place along the first side.

7. Leaving a 2" tail for later use, begin sewing the binding to the quilt with a ¼" seam.

For Mitered Corners:

1. Stop ¼" from the first corner. Leave the needle in the quilt and turn it 90°. Hit the reverse button on your machine and back off the quilt leaving the threads connected.

2. Fold the binding perpendicular to the side you sewed, making a 45° angle. Carefully maintaining the first fold, bring the binding back along the edge to be sewn.

3. Carefully align the edges of the binding with the quilt edge and sew as you did the first side. Repeat this process until you reach the tail left at the beginning. Fold the tail out of the way and sew until you are ¼" from the beginning stitches.

4. Remove the quilt from the machine. Fold the quilt out of the way and match the binding tails together. Carefully sew the binding tails with a ¼" seam. You can do this by hand if you prefer.

Finishing the Binding:

5. Trim the seam to reduce bulk.

6. Finish stitching the binding to the quilt across the join you just sewed.

7. Turn the binding to the back of the quilt. To reduce bulk at the corners, fold the miter in the opposite direction from which it was folded on the front.

8. Hand-sew a Blind stitch on the back of the quilt to secure the binding in place.

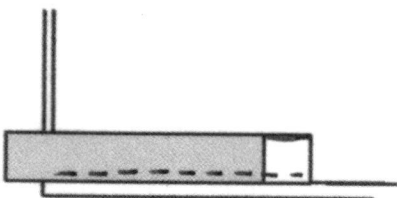

Align the raw edge of the binding with the raw edge of the quilt top. Start about 8" from the corner and go along the first side with a ¼" seam.

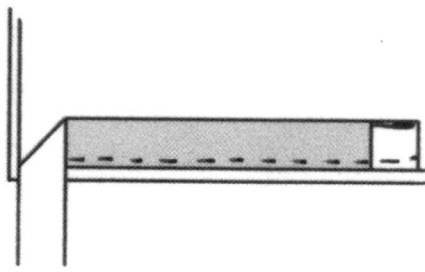

Stop ¼" from the edge. Then stitch a slant to the corner (through both layers of binding)... lift up, then down, as you line up the edge. Fold the binding back.

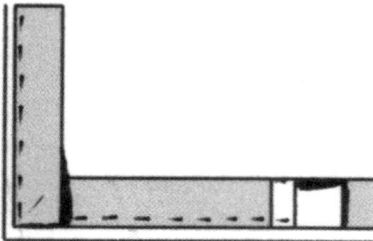

Align the raw edge again. Continue stitching the next side with a ¼" seam as you sew the binding in place.

Simply Strips & Squares

'Swell' Simple Blocks Quilt

photo is on page 49

SIZE: 54" x 66"

YARDAGE:
We used a *Moda* "Swell" by Urban Chiks
   'Jelly Roll' collection of 2½" fabric strips
   - we purchased 1 'Jelly Roll'
   ⅙ yard Red   OR   2 strips
   ¼ yard Green   OR   3 strips
   ¼ yard Pink   OR   3 strips
   ⅙ yard Yellow   OR   2 strips
   ⅙ yard Blue   OR   2 strips
   1⅝ yard Ivory   OR   22 strips
Border #1   Purchase ¼ yard Red
Border #4 & Binding   Purchase 1⅙ yards Green
Backing   Purchase 2⅞ yards
Batting   Purchase 62" x 74"
Sewing machine, needle, thread

PREPARATION FOR BLOCK A:
For Block Center pieces #1, #2, #3, & #4:
   Cut 8 Red strips 2½" x 8½" (for 2 blocks).
   Cut 12 Pink strips 2½" x 8½" (for 3 blocks).
   Cut 8 Yellow strips 2½" x 8½" (for 2 blocks).
   Cut 8 Blue strips 2½" x 8½" (for 2 blocks).
   Cut 12 Green strips 2½" x 8½" (for 3 blocks).
For Ivory surrounds:
   For #5 & #6: Cut 24 strips 2½" x 8½".
   For #7 & #8: Cut 24 strips 2½" x 12½".

SEW BLOCKS:
For each block, sew 4 strips as shown in the Block diagram. Press.
Sew #5 and #6 to the block. Press.
Sew #7 and #8 to the block. Press.
Each block will measure 12½" x 12½" at this point.

ASSEMBLY:
   Arrange all Blocks on a work surface or table.
   Refer to diagram for block placement and direction.
   Sew blocks together in 4 rows, 3 blocks per row. Press.
   Sew rows together. Press.

ADD THE BORDERS:
Border #1:
   Cut 5 Red 1½" strips and sew together end to end.
   Cut 2 strips 1½" x 48½" for sides.
   Cut 2 strips 1½" x 38½" for top and bottom.
   Sew side borders to the quilt. Press.
   Sew top and bottom borders to the quilt. Press.
Pieced Border #2:
   Sew 5 Ivory strips end to end.
   Cut 2 strips 2½" x 50½" for sides.
   Cut 2 strips 2½" x 42½" for top and bottom.
   Sew side borders to the quilt. Press.
   Sew top and bottom borders to the quilt. Press.
Pieced Border #3:
   Sew 5 Ivory strips end to end.
   Cut 2 strips 2½" x 54½" for sides.
   Cut 2 strips 2½" x 46½" for top and bottom.
   Sew side borders to the quilt. Press.
   Sew top and bottom borders to the quilt. Press.

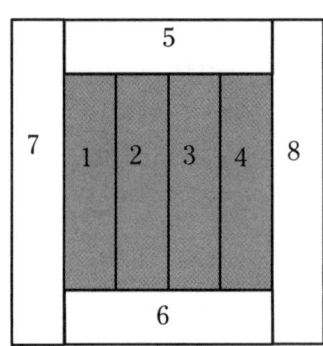

Block A
Make 2 Red, 3 Pink, 2 Yellow, 2 Blue, 3 Green

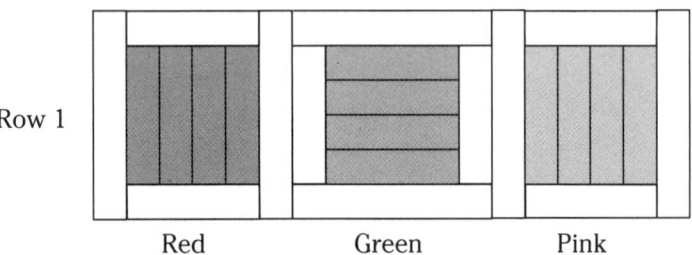

Row 1 — Red, Green, Pink

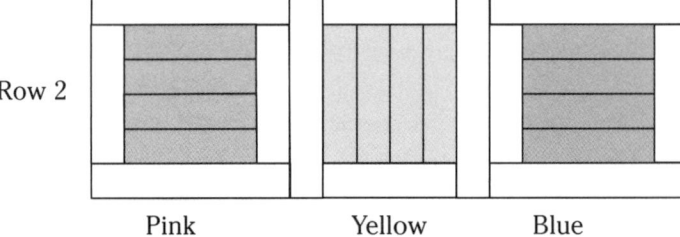

Row 2 — Pink, Yellow, Blue

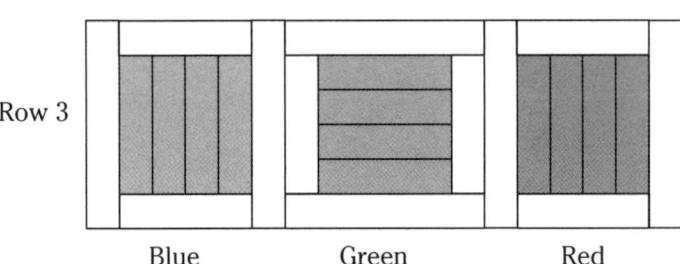

Row 3 — Blue, Green, Red

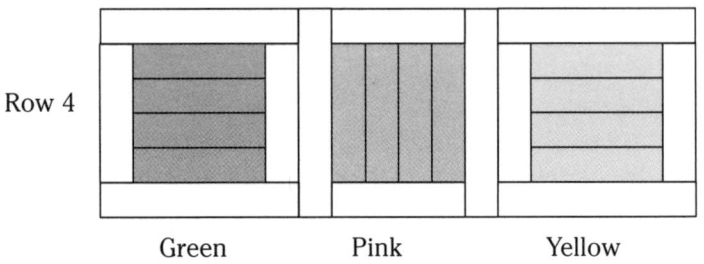

Row 4 — Green, Pink, Yellow

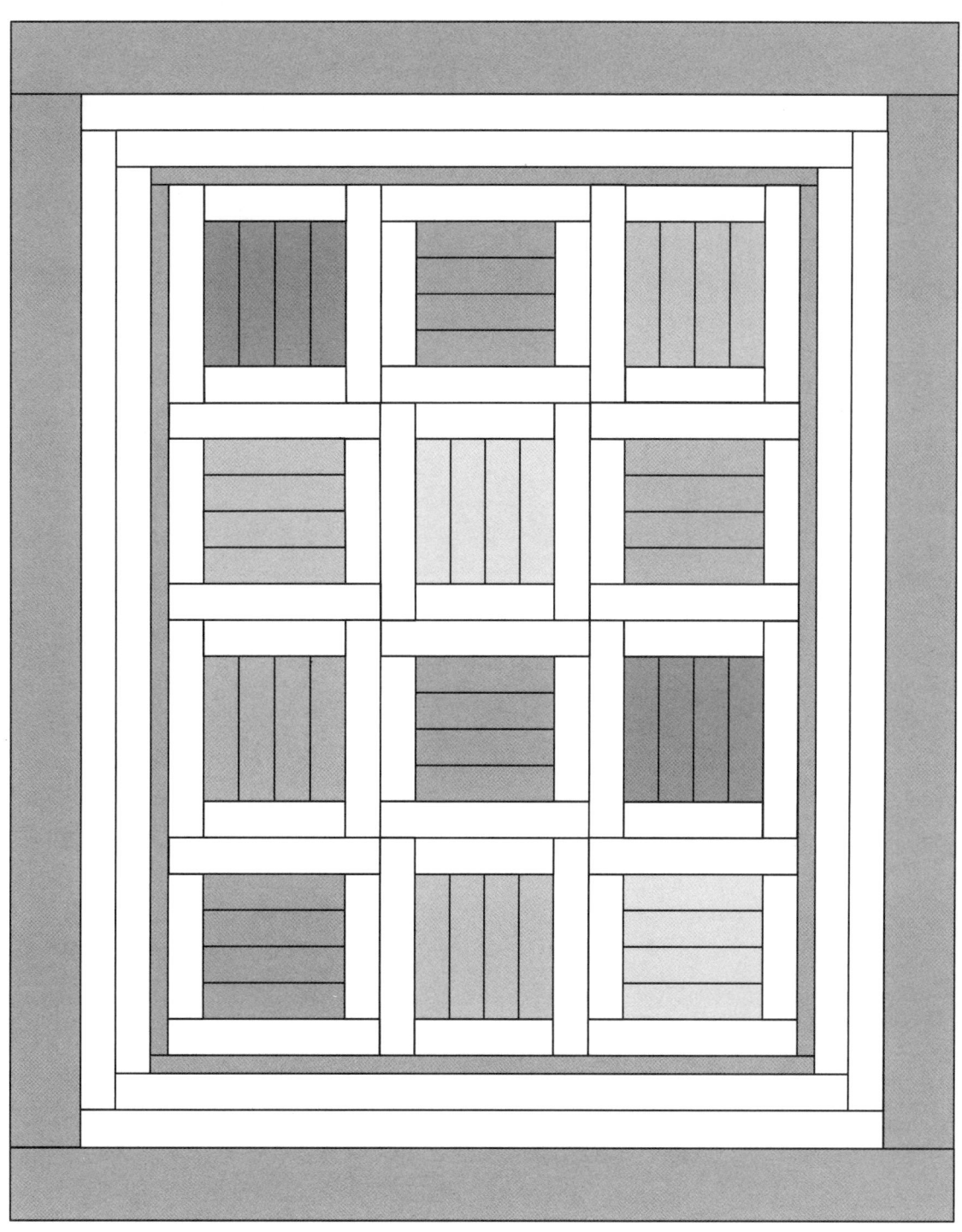

Outer Border #4:
Cut 6 Green 4½" strips.
Sew strips together end to end.
Cut 2 strips 4½" x 58½" for sides.
Cut 2 strips 4½" x 54½" for top and bottom.
Sew side borders to the quilt. Press.
Sew top and bottom borders to the quilt. Press.

FINISHING:
Quilting: See Basic Instructions on pages 26 - 28.
Binding: Cut six 2½" strips.
Sew together end to end to equal 248".
See Binding Instructions on page 29.

'Swell' Baby and Toddler Quilts
Two for the Price of One!

Use one 'Jelly Roll' to make two colorful quilts. Begin by dividing the colored strips into "girl" colors, and "boy" colors, then sew the strips in simple blocks. Charming and simple.

Basic Instructions for Girl & Boy
SEW BLOCKS:
For each block, sew center pieces #1 and #2 together. Press.
Sew #3 and #4 to the center of each block. Press.
Sew #5 and #6 to each block. Press.
Each block will measure 8½" x 8½" at this point.

ASSEMBLY:
Arrange all Blocks on a work surface or table.
Refer to diagram for block placement and direction.
Sew blocks together in 4 rows, 3 blocks per row. Press.
Sew rows together. Press.

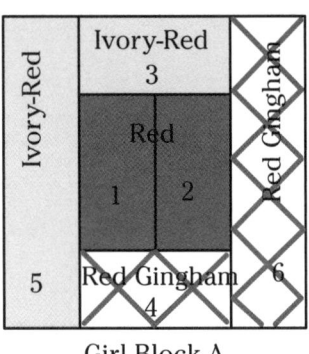
Girl Block A

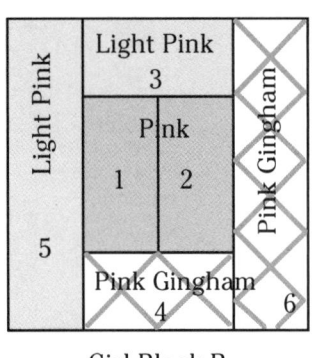
Girl Block B

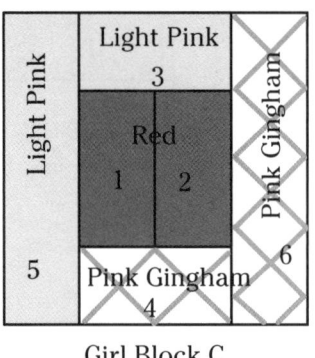
Girl Block C

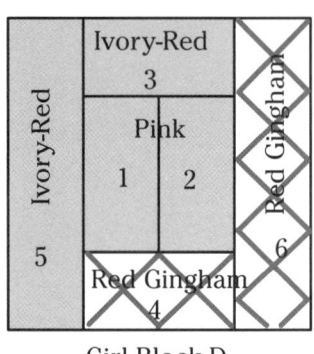
Girl Block D

A 'Swell' Girl
photo is on pages 48-49

SIZE: 34" x 42"

YARDAGE:
We used a Moda "Swell" by Urban Chiks
  'Jelly Roll' collection of 2½" fabric strips
  - we purchased 1 'Jelly Roll' (½ for girl quilt)
  ⅙ yard Red   OR   2 strips
  ⅙ yard Ivory/Red   OR   2 strips
  ⅙ yard Red Gingham   OR   2 strips
  ⅛ yard Pink   OR   1 strip
  ⅙ yard Lt Pink   OR   2 strips
  ⅙ yard Pink Gingham   OR   2 strips
Border #1   Purchase ⅛ yard Red
Border #2 & Binding
                  Purchase 1 yard Pink Gingham
Backing   Purchase 1½ yards
Batting   Purchase 42" x 50"
Sewing machine, needle, thread

PREPARATION FOR BLOCKS A, B, C, AND D:
For 4 Block A's:
  Cut 8 Red strips 2½" x 4½" for #1 and #2.
  Cut 4 Ivory-Red strips 2½" x 4½" for #3.
  Cut 4 Red Gingham strips 2½" x 4½" for #4.
  Cut 4 Ivory-Red strips 2½" x 8½" for #5.
  Cut 4 Red Gingham strips 2½" x 8½" for #6.
For 2 Block B's:
  Cut 4 Pink strips 2½" x 4½" for #1 and #2.
  Cut 2 Light Pink strips 2½" x 4½" for #3.
  Cut 2 Pink Gingham strips 2½" x 4½" for #4.
  Cut 2 Light Pink strips 2½" x 8½" for #5.
  Cut 2 Pink Gingham strips 2½" x 8½" for #6.
For 4 Block C's:
  Cut 8 Red strips 2½" x 4½" for #1 and #2.
  Cut 4 Light Pink strips 2½" x 4½" for #3.
  Cut 4 Pink Gingham strips 2½" x 4½" for #4.
  Cut 4 Light Pink strips 2½" x 8½" for #5.
  Cut 4 Pink Gingham strips 2½" x 8½" for #6.

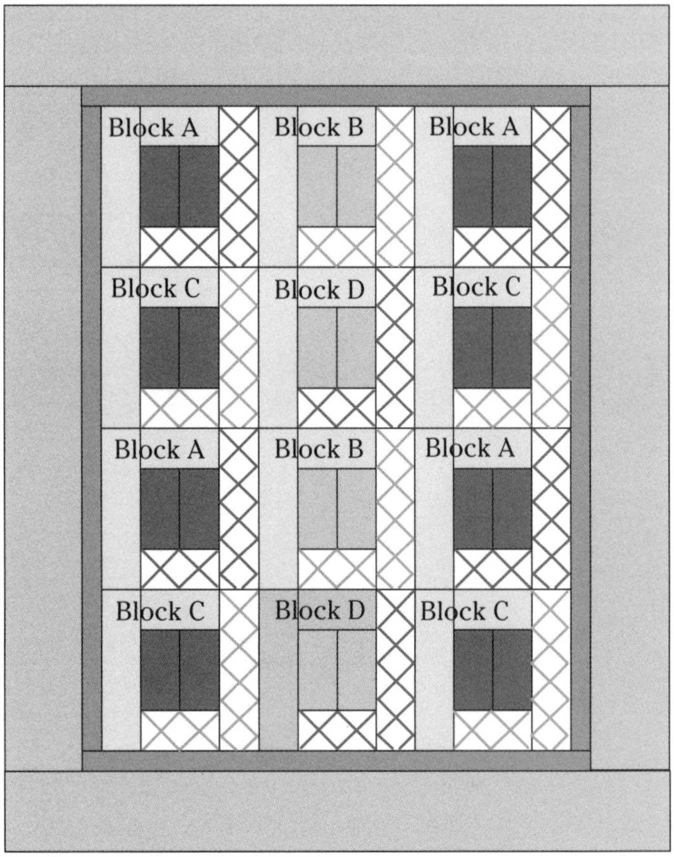

For 2 Block D's:
  Cut 4 Pink strips 2½" x 4½" for #1 and #2.
  Cut 2 Ivory-Red strips 2½" x 4½" for #3.
  Cut 2 Red Gingham strips 2½" x 4½" for #4.
  Cut 2 Ivory-Red strips 2½" x 8½" for #5.
  Cut 2 Red Gingham strips 2½" x 8½" for #6.

ADD THE BORDERS:
Inner Border #1:
Cut 1½" strips.
Cut 2 strips 1½" x 32½" for sides.
Cut 2 strips 1½" x 26½" for top and bottom.
Sew side borders to the quilt. Press.
Sew top and bottom borders to the quilt. Press.

Outer Border #2:
Cut 4½" strips.
Cut 2 strips 4½" x 34½" for sides.
Cut 2 strips 4½" x 34½" for top and bottom.
Sew side borders to the quilt. Press.
Sew top and bottom borders to the quilt. Press.

FINISHING:
Quilting:
See Basic Instructions on pages 26 - 28.
Binding:
Cut four 2½" strips.
Sew together end to end to equal 160".
See Binding Instructions on page 29.

A 'Swell' Boy

photo is on page 48-49

SIZE: 34" x 42"
YARDAGE:
We used a Moda "Swell" by Urban Chiks
　'Jelly Roll' collection of 2½" fabric strips
　- we purchased 1 'Jelly Roll' (½ for boy quilt)
　⅙ yard Green　　　　　OR　2 strips
　⅙ yard Ivory/Green　　　OR　2 strips
　⅙ yard Green Gingham　OR　2 strips
　⅛ yard Blue　　　　　　OR　1 strip
　⅙ yard Lt Blue　　　　　OR　2 strips
　⅙ yard Blue Gingham　　OR　2 strips
Border #1　　　Purchase ⅛ yard Green
Border #2 & Binding
　　　　　　　Purchase 1 yard Blue Gingham
Backing　　　　Purchase 1½ yards
Batting　　　　Purchase 42" x 50"
Sewing machine, needle, thread

PREPARATION FOR BLOCKS A, B, C, AND D:
For 4 Block A's:
　Cut 8 Green strips 2½" x 4½" for #1 and #2.
　Cut 4 Ivory-Green strips 2½" x 4½" for #3.
　Cut 4 Green Gingham strips 2½" x 4½" for #4.
　Cut 4 Ivory-Green strips 2½" x 8½" for #5.
　Cut 4 Green Gingham strips 2½" x 8½" for #6.
For 2 Block B's:
　Cut 4 Blue strips 2½" x 4½" for #1 and #2.
　Cut 2 Light Blue strips 2½" x 4½" for #3.
　Cut 2 Blue Gingham strips 2½" x 4½" for #4.
　Cut 2 Light Blue strips 2½" x 8½" for #5.
　Cut 2 Blue Gingham strips 2½" x 8½" for #6.
For 4 Block C's:
　Cut 8 Green strips 2½" x 4½" for #1 and #2.
　Cut 4 Light Blue strips 2½" x 4½" for #3.
　Cut 4 Blue Gingham strips 2½" x 4½" for #4.
　Cut 4 Light Blue strips 2½" x 8½" for #5.
　Cut 4 Blue Gingham strips 2½" x 8½" for #6.

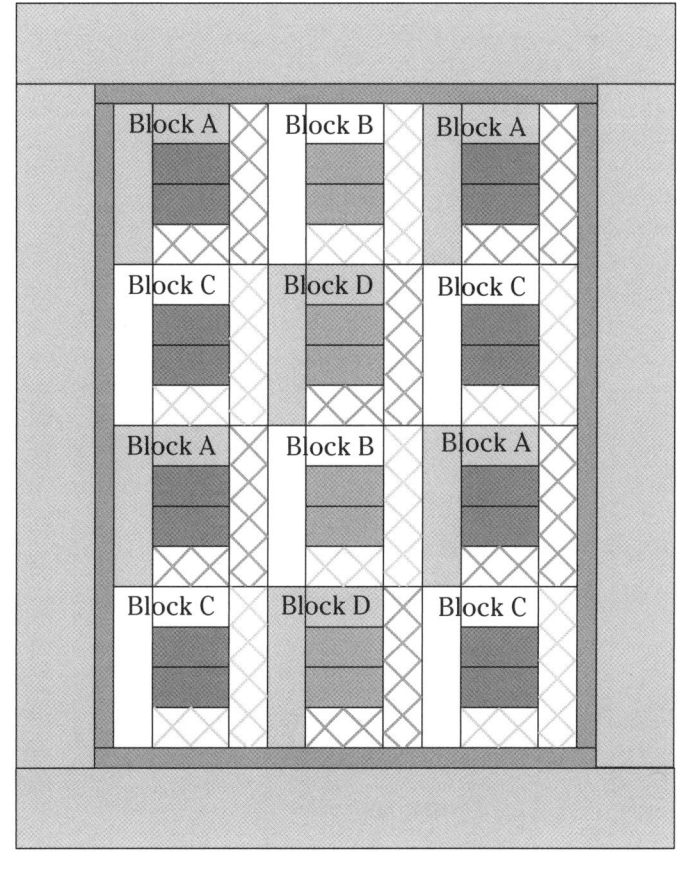

For 2 Block D's:
　Cut 4 Blue strips 2½" x 4½" for #1 and #2.
　Cut 2 Ivory-Green strips 2½" x 4½" for #3.
　Cut 2 Green Gingham strips 2½" x 4½" for #4.
　Cut 2 Ivory-Green strips 2½" x 8½" for #5.
　Cut 2 Green Gingham strips 2½" x 8½" for #6.

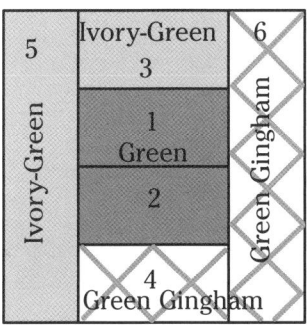
Boy Block A

Boy Block B

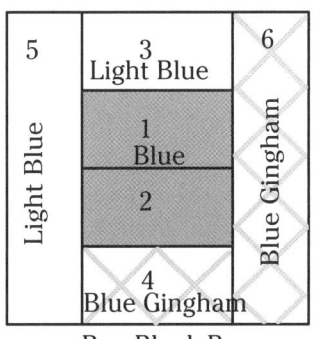

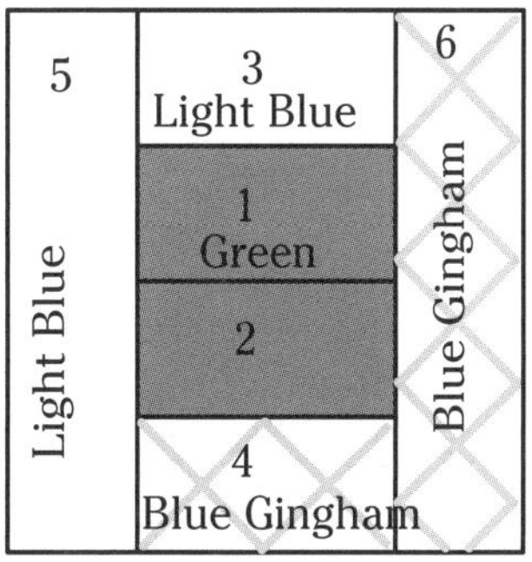

Boy Block C

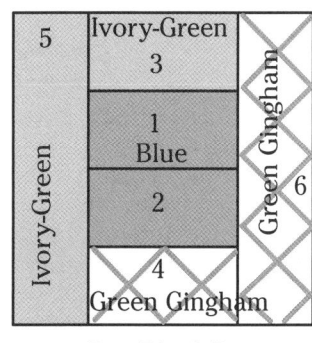
Boy Block D

Flutterby

photo on page 50 - 51

SIZE: 60" x 68"

YARDAGE:
We used a *Moda* "Flutterby" by Tula Pink
  'Jelly Roll' collection of 2½" fabric strips
  - we purchased 1 'Jelly Roll'
  ⅛ yard Gold/Yellow OR 1 strip
  ¼ yard Red   OR 2 strips
  ⅜ yard Pink   OR 5 strips
  ½ yard Brown   OR 7 strips
  ¾ yard Green   OR 10 strips
  ¼ yard Ivory   OR 3 strips
  ¾ yard Aqua   OR 10 strips
Border #1   Purchase ¼ yard Brown
Border #2 & Binding   Purchase 1½ yards Pink
Backing   Purchase 3⅝ yards
Batting   Purchase 68" x 76"
Sewing machine, needle, thread
DMC Dark Brown pearl cotton, Chenille needle

PREPARATION FOR BLOCKS
These instructions are arranged to allow you to cut the longest pieces first.
Use 2½" wide strips.

Cut these Green strips:
  six 34½" for Block L,
  two 30½" for Block M,
  two 18½" and two 4½" for Block H,
  five 8½", three 6½", four 4½", ten 2½".
Cut these Pink strips:
  two 24½", two 16½", six 8½", ten 6½", two 4½".
Cut these Red strips:
  four 8½", four 6½", four 4½", four** 2½".
  **TIP: You'll probably need to cut one square from a Pink strip that has a lot of Red print.
Cut these Gold strips:
  four 4½", two 2½"
Cut a Brown strip
  one 16½" long for the center body.

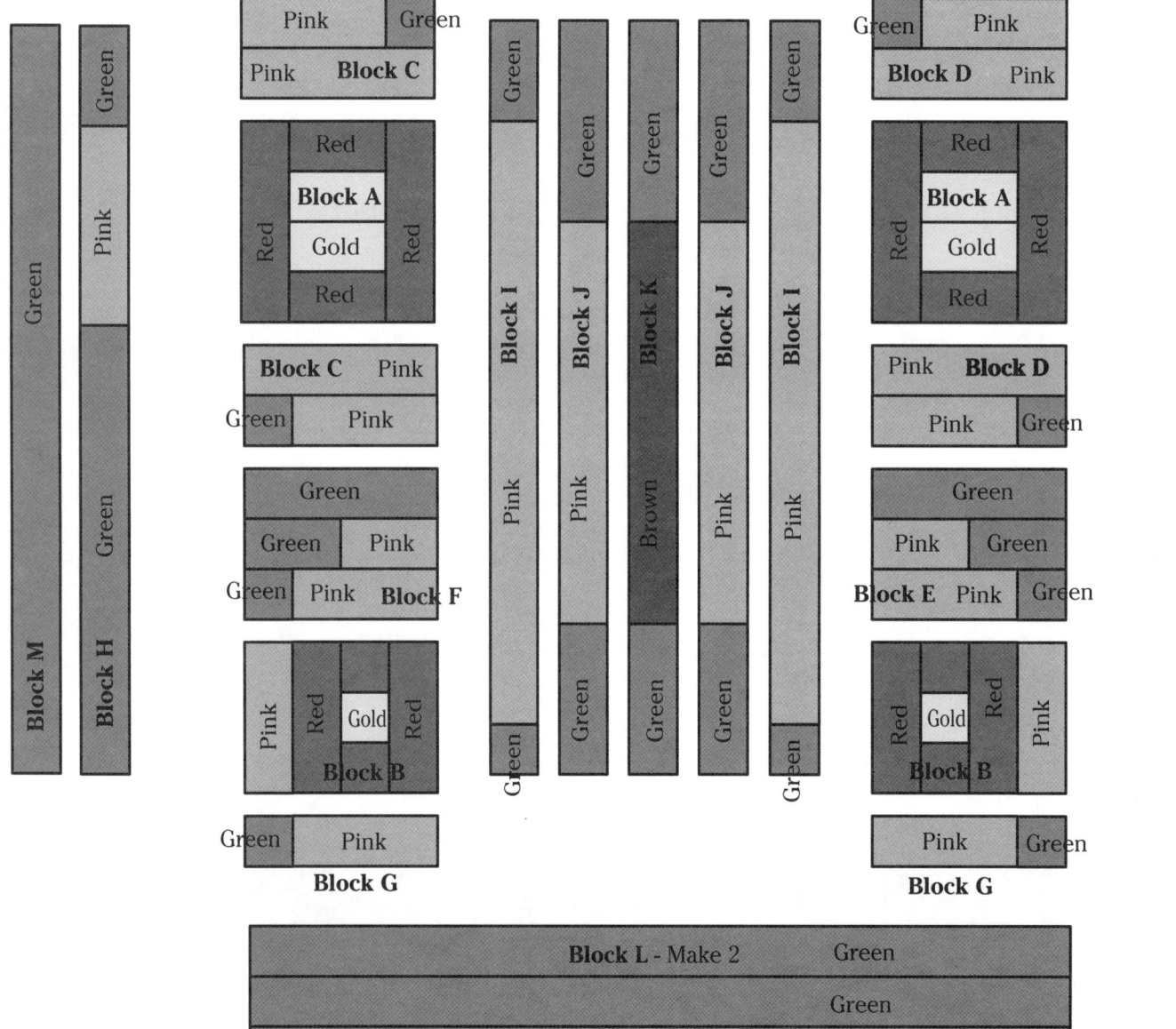

34 *Simply Strips & Squares*

SEW BLOCKS:
Arrange the pieces following the block diagrams.
Block A:
  Sew a column of 4½" strips: Red-Gold-Gold-Red. Press.
  Sew a Red 8½" strip to each side.
    Press. Make 2.
Block B:
  Sew a column of 2½" strips: Red-Gold-Red. Press.
  Sew a Red 6½" strip to each side. Press.
  Sew a Pink 6½" strip to one side as shown in diagram.
    Press. Make 2.

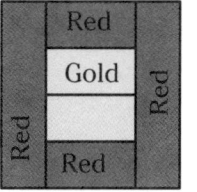
Block A Make 2

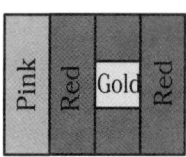
Block B Make 2

Block C:
  Sew a Pink 6½" strip to a Green 2½" square. Press.
  Sew a Pink 8½" strip to the bottom. Press.
  Make 2.
Block D:
  Sew a Green 2½" square to a Pink 6½" strip. Press.
  Sew a Pink 8½" strip to the bottom. Press.
  Make 2.

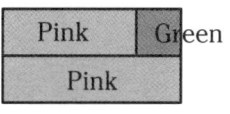
Block C Make 2

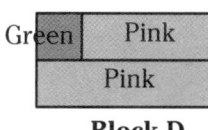
Block D Make 2

Block E:
  Row 1: You need a Green 8½" strip.
  Row 2: Sew a Pink 4½" strip to a Green 4½" strip. Press.
  Row 3: Sew a Pink 6½" strip to a Green 2½" square. Press.
  Sew the rows together. Press. Make 1.
Block F:
  Row 1: You need a Green 8½" strip.
  Row 2: Sew a Green 4½" strip to a Pink 4½" strip. Press.
  Row 3: Sew a Green 2½" square to a Pink 6½" strip. Press.
  Sew the rows together.
  Press. Make 1.

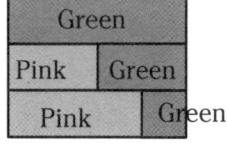
Block E Make 1

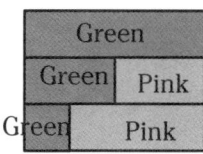
Block F Make 1

Block G:
  Sew a Green 2½" square to a Pink 6½" strip.
  Press. Make 2.

Block G Make 2

Block H:
  Sew a Green 18½" strip to a Pink 8½" strip to a Green 4½" strip.
  Press. Make 2.
Block I
  Sew a Green 2½" square to a Pink 24½" strip to a Green 4½" strip.
  Press. Make 2.
Block J:
  Sew a Green 6½" strip to a Pink 16½" strip to a Green 8½" strip.
  Press. Make 2.
Block K:
  Sew a Green 6½" strip to a Brown 16½" strip to a Green 8½" strip.
  Press. Make only 1.
Block L:
  Sew 3 Green strips together to make a piece 6½" x 34½"..
  Press. Make 2.
Block M:
  Use Green 30½" strips. You'll need 2.

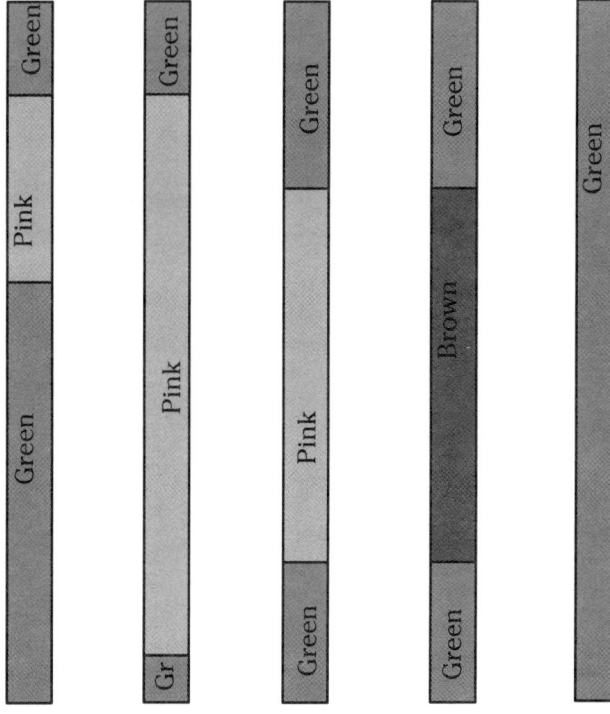

ASSEMBLY:
Arrange all Blocks on a work surface or table.
Refer to diagram for block placement and direction.
Sew blocks together in 7 columns. Press.
Sew the columns together. Press.
Embroider the antennae with Dark Brown
  pearl cotton and a chenille needle.

continued on page 36

Simply Strips & Squares 35

Flutterby - continued from page 35

Antennae to Embroider

Brown Pieced Border #1:
    Cut 2½" strips.
    Sew strips together end to end.
    Cut 2 strips 2½" x 34½" for top and bottom.
    Cut 2 strips 2½" x 46½" for sides.
    Sew top and bottom borders to the quilt. Press.
    Sew side borders to the quilt. Press.

Checkerboard Border #2:
    Use 2½" strips.
    Sew leftover Ivory strips together end to end to make a strip 52½" long.
    Sew leftover Brown strips together end to end to make a strip 52½" long.
    Sew the strips together side by side to make a piece 4½" x 52½".

    Cut the strips into 21 pieces 2½" x 4½".
    Sew 11 pieces end to end, Ivory-Brown-Ivory-Brown etc. for each side.

    Cut 2 Ivory and 2 Brown squares 2½" x 2½".
    Sew 1 Brown square to the last Ivory piece on each side.
    Sew side borders to the quilt. Press.

    Sew 10 pieces end to end, Ivory-Brown-Ivory-Brown, etc. for the top and bottom.
    Sew 1 Ivory square to the last Brown piece.
    Sew top and bottom borders to the quilt. Press.

Flutterby - Quilt Center Assembly

Aqua Pieced Border #3:
    Cut 2½" strips.
    Sew strips together end to end.
    Cut 2 strips 2½" x 50½" for sides.
    Cut 2 strips 2½" x 46½" for top and bottom.
    Sew side borders to the quilt. Press.
    Sew top and bottom borders to the quilt. Press.

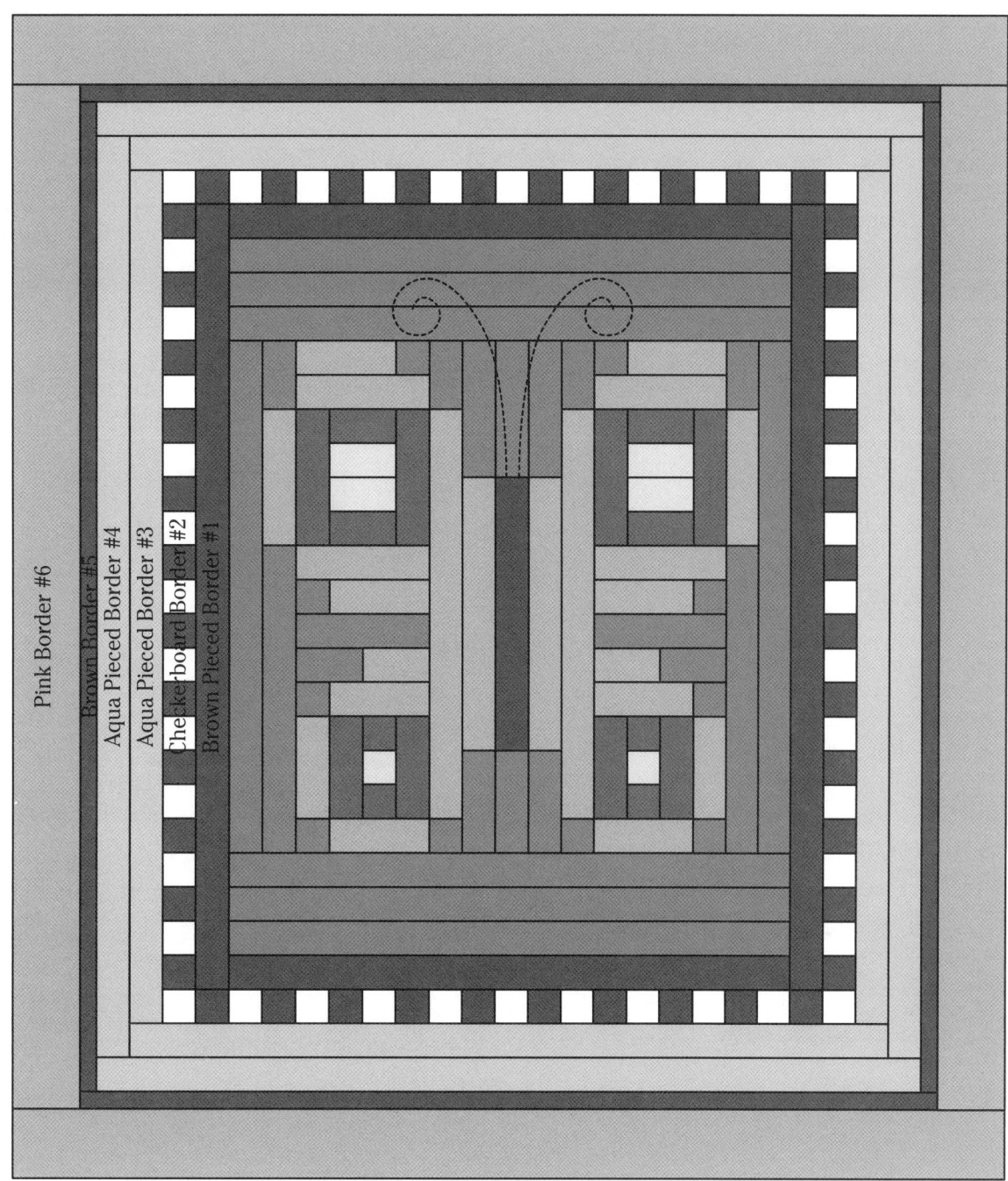

Flutterby
Quilt Assembly Diagram

Aqua Pieced Border #4:
Cut 2½" strips.
Sew strips together end to end.
Cut 2 strips 2½" x 54½" for sides.
Cut 2 strips 2½" x 50½" for top and bottom.
Sew side borders to the quilt. Press.
Sew top and bottom borders to the quilt. Press.

Brown Border #5:
Cut 1½" strips.
Sew strips together end to end.
Cut 2 strips 1½" x 58½" for sides.
Cut 2 strips 1½" x 52½" for top and bottom.
Sew side borders to the quilt. Press.
Sew top and bottom borders to the quilt. Press.

Pink Border #6
Cut 4½" strips.
Sew strips together end to end.
Cut 2 strips 4½" x 60½" for sides.
Cut 2 strips 4½" x 60½" for top and bottom.
Sew side borders to the quilt. Press.
Sew top and bottom borders to the quilt. Press.

FINISHING:
Quilting:
See Basic Instructions on pages 26 - 28.
Binding:
Cut seven 2½" strips.
Sew together end to end to equal 266".
See Binding Instructions on page 29.

Simply Strips & Squares

Through the Garden Gate

'Block of the Month'

A Morris Garden

photos on pages 46 - 47

SIZE: 52" x 68"

YARDAGE:

We used a *Moda* "A Morris Garden" by Barbara Brackman
'Jelly Roll' collection of 2½" fabric strips
- we purchased 1 'Jelly Roll'

⅓ yard Yellow/Gold	OR	4 strips
⅓ yard Olive Green	OR	4 strips
⅙ yard Navy/Black	OR	2 strips
½ yard Blue (Light to Medium)	OR	7 strips
⅓ yard Dark Blue	OR	3 strips
¼ yard Light Green	OR	3 strips
⅙ yard Tan with Blue	OR	2 strips
¼ yard Ivory print	OR	3 strips
½ yard Black print	OR	7 strips
⅙ yard Brown	OR	2 strips

Border #2   Purchase ¼ yard Black solid
Border #3 & Binding   Purchase 1¼ yards Black print
Backing   Purchase 3½ yards
Batting   Purchase 60" x 76"
Sewing machine, needle, thread
DMC pearl cotton (Dark Green, Green, Yellow), Chenille needle

PREPARATION For Blocks

A - SUN IN THE SKY:
Log Cabin:
Cut the following Gold strips:
   #3 - one 2½" x 4½".
   #5 - one 2½" x 6½".
   #7 & #8 - two 2½" x 8½".
Cut the following Light Blue strips:
   #1 & #2 - two 2½" x 4½".
   #4 - one 2½" x 6½".
   #6 - one 2½" x 8½".
   #9, #10, & #11 - three 2½" x 12½".
Sew strip 1 to 2. Press.
Sew strip 3 to the top of 1-2. Press.
Sew strip 4 to the side. Press.
Sew strip 5 to the top. Press.
Sew strip 6 to the side. Press.
Sew strips 7 and 8 to the top. Press.
Sew strips 9, 10, and 11 to the side. Press.
This is the first block of Row 1 and measures 12½" x 14½".

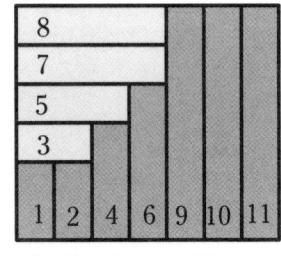

A - Sun in the Sky
Log Cabin

B - SKY AND FLOWERS on the horizon:
Checkerboard:
Cut 3 Light Blue strips 2½" x 24½".
Sew these strips together to make a piece 6½" wide. Press.
This piece will be sewn to the top of the checkerboard.
Cut 3 Yellow/Gold strips and 3 Light Blue strips 15" long.
Sew 3 strips together Yellow/Gold - Blue - Yellow/Gold to make
   a piece 6½" wide. Press.
Sew 3 strips together Blue - Yellow/Gold - Blue to make
   a piece 6½" wide. Press.
Cut each strip into 6 pieces each 2½" wide.
Arrange the strips in a checkerboard as shown in the
   diagram.
Sew the strips together. Press.
Sew the 3 Light Blue strips to the top. Press.
This is the second block in Row 1 and measures 12½" x 24½".

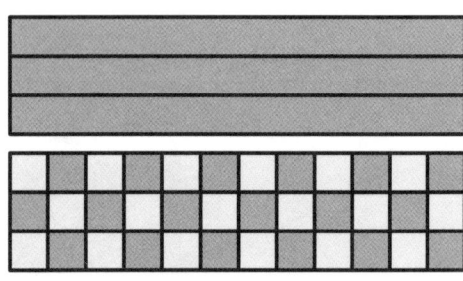

Checkerboard

Sew Sections together for Row 1:
Sew Sections A and B together to complete Row 1.

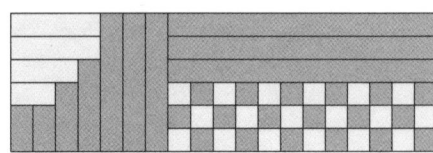

Row 1

C - TREES ON THE HORIZON:
Tree Tops:
Cut 6 Light Green strips 2½" x 6½" for #5 Tree Tops.
Sew 3 Light Green strips together to make a piece 6½" wide.
   Press.
Make 2.

'Snowball' Mitered Corners:
Cut 8 Dark Blue squares 2½" x 2½".
Position each square on a corner of the Green square
   as shown.
Sew on the diagonal.
Fold back the triangles to cover the corners. Press.
Trim off extra fabric underneath the triangle.

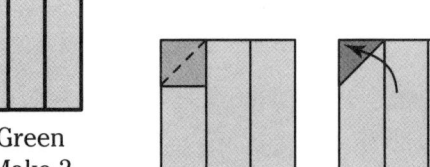 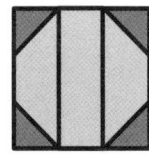

Green
Make 2

Dark Blue Corners
Cut 8

Tree Tops

Tree Top
Make 2

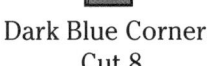

Background Sky and Tree Assembly
    Cut 2 Dark Blue strips 2½" x 6½" for top of block.
    Cut 4 Dark Blue strips 2½" x 4½" for trunk section.
    Cut 2 Brown strips 2½" x 4½" for trunk.
    Sew the trunk pieces together. Press.
    Sew the trunk section to the bottom of the Tree Top section. Press.
    Sew a Dark Blue strip to the top of the Tree Top section. Press.

Tree Block
    Cut 2 Medium Blue strips 2½" x 12½".
    Cut 3 Dark Blue strips 2½" x 12½".
    Sew a Medium Blue strip - Dark Blue strip - Tree block - Dark Blue strip -
        Tree block - Dark Blue strip - Medium Blue strip. Press.
    This is the top portion of the first block on Row 2 and measures 12½" x 22½".

D - FLOWER ROWS BELOW THE TREES:
Vertical Stripes:
    Cut 1 Gold and 3 Olive strips 2½" x 22½".
    Cut 1 Olive strip 2½" x 4½".
    Sew 1 Olive to 1 Gold strip to make a piece 4½" wide. Press.
    Set aside the other 2 Olive strips for the top and bottom border.
    Cut the Olive-Gold strip into 5 pieces 4½" x 4½".
    Arrange the pieces Olive-Gold-Olive-Gold as shown in the diagram.
    Sew the pieces together, adding the single Olive strip at the end. Press.
    Sew a 22½" Olive strip above and below the vertical stripes. Press.
    Sew the stripe section to the bottom of the tree block.
    This completes the first block of Row 2 and measures 20½" x 22½".

E - HOUSE BLOCK:
House:
    #1, 3 & 5 - Cut 3 Brown strips 2½" x 4½".
    #2 & 4 - Cut 2 Gold strips 2½" x 4½".
    #6 & 7 - Cut 2 Brown strips 2½" x 10½".
    #8, 9 - Cut 2 Navy/Black strips 2½" x 8½".
    #10 - Cut 1 Brown strip 2½" x 8½".
    #11 - Cut 1 Brown strip 2½" x 16½".
    #12 - Cut 1 Navy/Black strip 2½" x 16½".
    #13 & 15 - Cut 2 Brown squares 2½" x 2½".
    #14, 17 & 18 - Cut 3 Medium Blue strips 2½" x 4½".
    #16 - Cut 1 Navy/Black strip 2½" x 8½".
    #19 - Cut 1 Navy/Black strip 2½" x 12½".
    #20 & 21 - Cut 2 Medium Blue strips 2½" x 6½".
    #22 - Cut 1 Medium Blue strip 2½" x 16½".
    Sew #1 to 2 to 3 to 4 to 5. Press.
    Sew 6 - 7 to the bottom of 1-5. Press.
    Sew #8 to 9 to 10. Press.
    Sew 8-9-10 to the left side of 1-7. Press.
    Sew #11 and #12 to the top of the block. Press.
    Set aside. This is the bottom of the house.
    Sew #13 to 14 to 15. Press.
    Sew #16 to the bottom of 13-14-15. Press.
    Sew # 17 and #18 to the sides. Press.
    Sew #19 to the bottom of the block. Press.
    Sew # 20 and #21 to the sides of the block. Press.
    Sew #22 to the top of the block.
    Sew the block to the bottom section of the house. Press.
        The house is the second block in Row 2 and measures
        16½" x 20½"

Sew Sections Together for Row 2:
    Sew Sections C, D and E together to complete Row 2.

continued on page 40

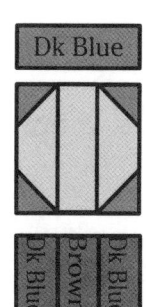

Tree Assembly
Make 2

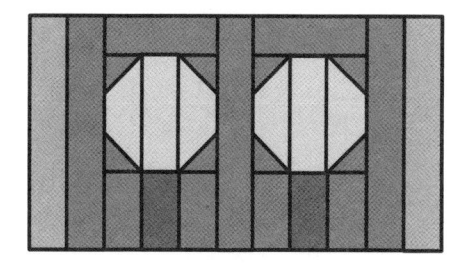

Tree Block

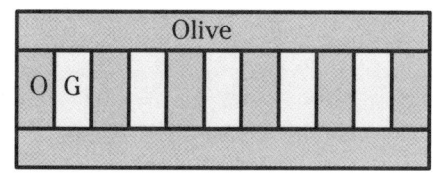

Stripe Section

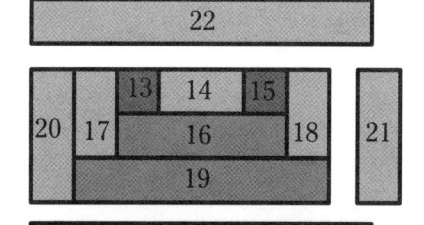

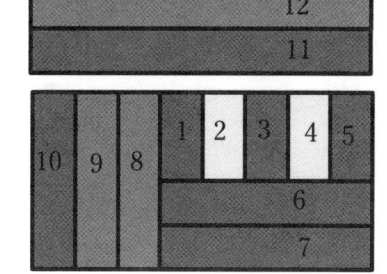

House

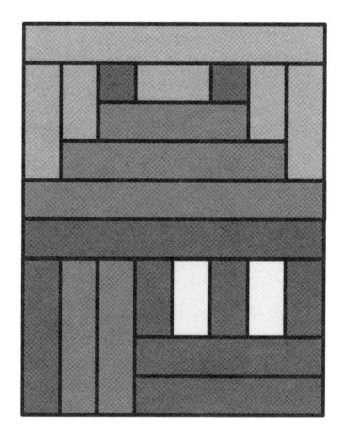

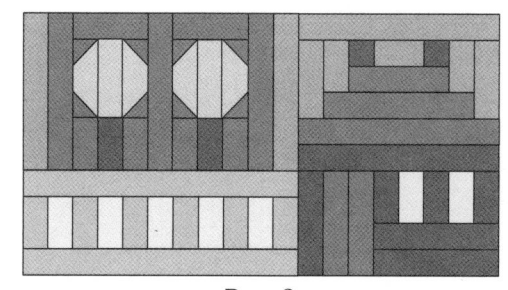

Row 2

Simply Strips & Squares 39

Through the Garden Gate - continued from page 39

F - MAKE THE GARDEN GATE:
Gate: and Door:
- Cut 4 Black print strips 2½" x 18½" for door.
- Cut 2 Ivory strips 2½" x 18½" for door frame sides.
- Cut 1 Ivory strip 2½" x 12½" for top of door frame.
- Cut 2 Olive Green strips 2½" x 8½" for left side of door.
- Cut 1 Light Blue, 3 Tan, and 2 Ivory strips 2½" x 4½" for left side of door.
- Cut 1 Light Green strip 2½" x 16½" for bottom of door.
- Sew the Black print door strips together to make a piece 8½" x 18½". Press.
- Sew the Ivory door frame sides to the door. Press.
- Sew the Ivory door frame top in place. Press.

Left Side Section:
- Sew the 2 Olive Green strips together to make a piece 4½" x 8½".
- Sew the 4½" pieces together to make a piece 12½" long:
    Light Blue-Tan-Ivory-Tan-Ivory-Tan. Press.
- Sew this piece to the bottom of the Olive Green section. Press.
- Sew this section to the left side of the door. Press.

Bottom:
- Sew the Light Green strip to the bottom of the door. Press.

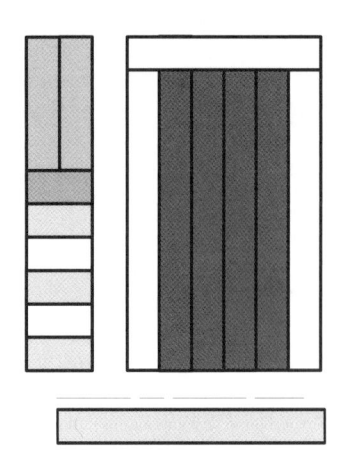

G - CONSTRUCT THE FLOWERS:
Pinwheel Flowers:
- Cut 2 Yellow/Gold strips 2½" x 18½". Sew together side by side.
- Cut 2 Olive Green strips 2½" x 18½" and sew together side by side.
- Cut each piece into 4 squares 4½" x 4½".
- With right sides together, make 4 pairs of Gold and Olive Green.
- Follow the Half-Square Triangle instructions on page 41.
- Trim each half-square triangle to 3½" x 3½".
- Position the pieces following the diagram and sew
    2 pinwheel blocks. Press.
- Cut 5 Olive Green strips 2½" x 6½".
- Cut 1 Olive Green and 1 Light Green strip 2½" x 22½".
- Sew 2 Olive Green strips, 1 pinwheel, 1 Olive Green strip,
    1 pinwheel, 2 Olive Green strips. Press.
- Sew an Olive Green strip to the top of this pieces and a Light Green
    strip to the bottom. Press.

H - ASSEMBLE THE FENCE:
Picket Fence:
- Cut 3 Ivory strips 2½" x 10½" for the fence.
- Cut 1 Tan strip 2½" x 22½" to place below the fence.
- Cut the following 2½" x 4½" strips: 6 Tan, 8 Ivory, 4 Light Blue, 2 Green.
- Sew the following 4 pieces 4½" x 10½" and press:
    Section A: Tan-Ivory-Tan-Ivory-Light Blue
    Section B: Light Blue-Ivory-Tan-Ivory-Green
    Section C: Tan-Ivory-Light Blue-Ivory-Tan
    Section D: Light Blue-Ivory-Tan-Ivory-Green
- Sew a row of A-Ivory-B-Ivory-C-Ivory-D. Press.
- Sew the Tan strip to the bottom of the piece. Press.
- Sew this section to the bottom of the Pinwheel section. Press.

Sew Sections together for Row 3
- Sew Sections F, G and H together to complete Row 3.

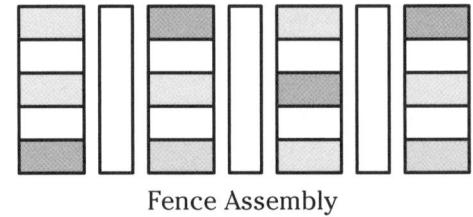

Gate and Door

Half-Square triangle Make 8

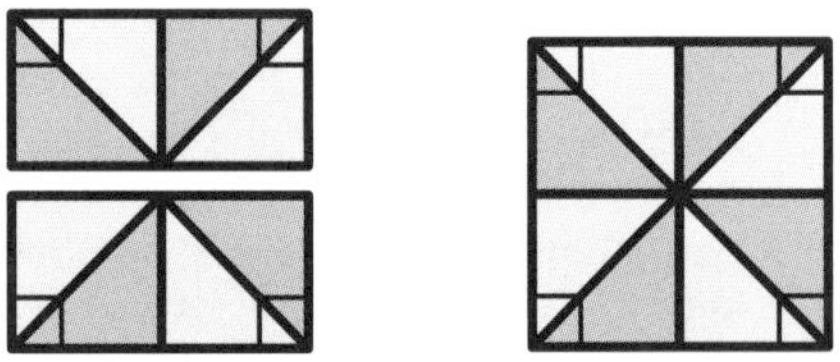

Pinwheel Flowers - Make 2

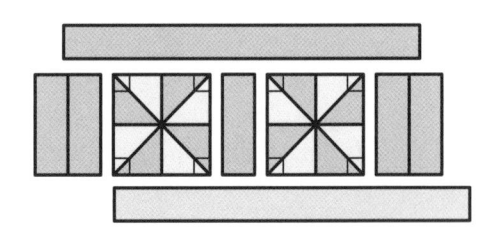

Pinwheel Block Assembly

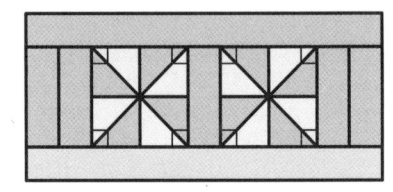

Pinwheel Flowers Block

Fence Assembly

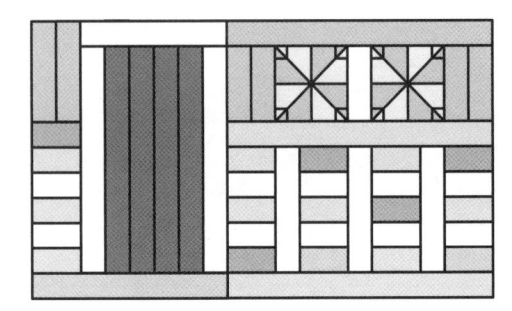

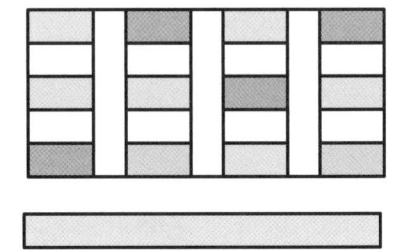

Fence Block

Row 3

40 *Simply Strips & Squares*

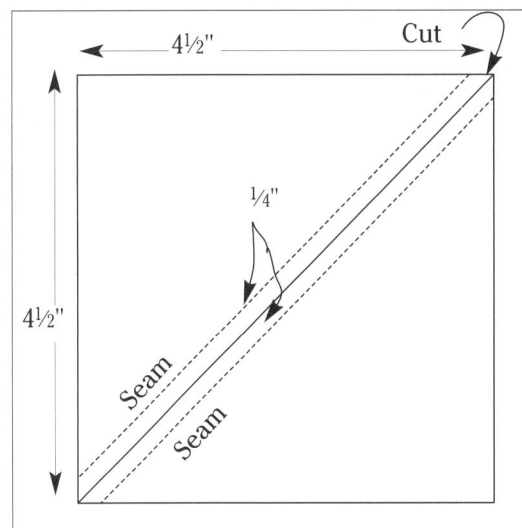

Half-Square Triangle Diagram
1. Place 2 squares right sides together.
2. Draw a diagonal line from corner to corner.
3. Stitch ¼" on each side of the line.
4. Cut squares apart on the diagonal line.
5. Open the 2 new squares with 2 colors.
6. Press. Trim off dog-ears.
7. Trim to 3½" x 3½".

ASSEMBLY:
Arrange all Rows and Blocks on a work surface or table.
Sew Rows 1, 2 and 3 together. Press.

Pieced Border #1:
Use Black print 2½" strips. Cut strips into random pieces.
Sew strips together end to end.
 Cut 2 strips 2½" x 54½" long for sides.
 Cut 2 strips 2½" x42½" long for top and bottom.
Sew side borders to the quilt. Press.
Sew top and bottom borders to the quilt. Press.

continued on page 42

Simply Strips & Squares 41

Through the Garden Gate - Quilt Assembly Diagram

Border #2:
Cut 1½" strips.
Sew strips together end to end.
    Cut 2 strips 1½" x 58½" for sides.
    Cut 2 strips 1½" x 44½" for top and bottom.
    Sew side borders to the quilt. Press.
    Sew top and bottom borders to the quilt. Press.

Border #3:
Cut 4½" strips.
Sew strips together end to end.
    Cut 2 strips 4½" x 60½" for sides.
    Cut 2 strips 4½" x 52½" for top and bottom.
    Sew side borders to the quilt. Press.
    Sew top and bottom borders to the quilt. Press.

FINISHING:
Quilting:
    See Basic Instructions on pages 26 - 28.
Binding:
    Cut seven 2½" strips.
    Sew together end to end to equal 248".
    See Binding Instructions on page 29.

Through the Garden Gate - continued from page 41

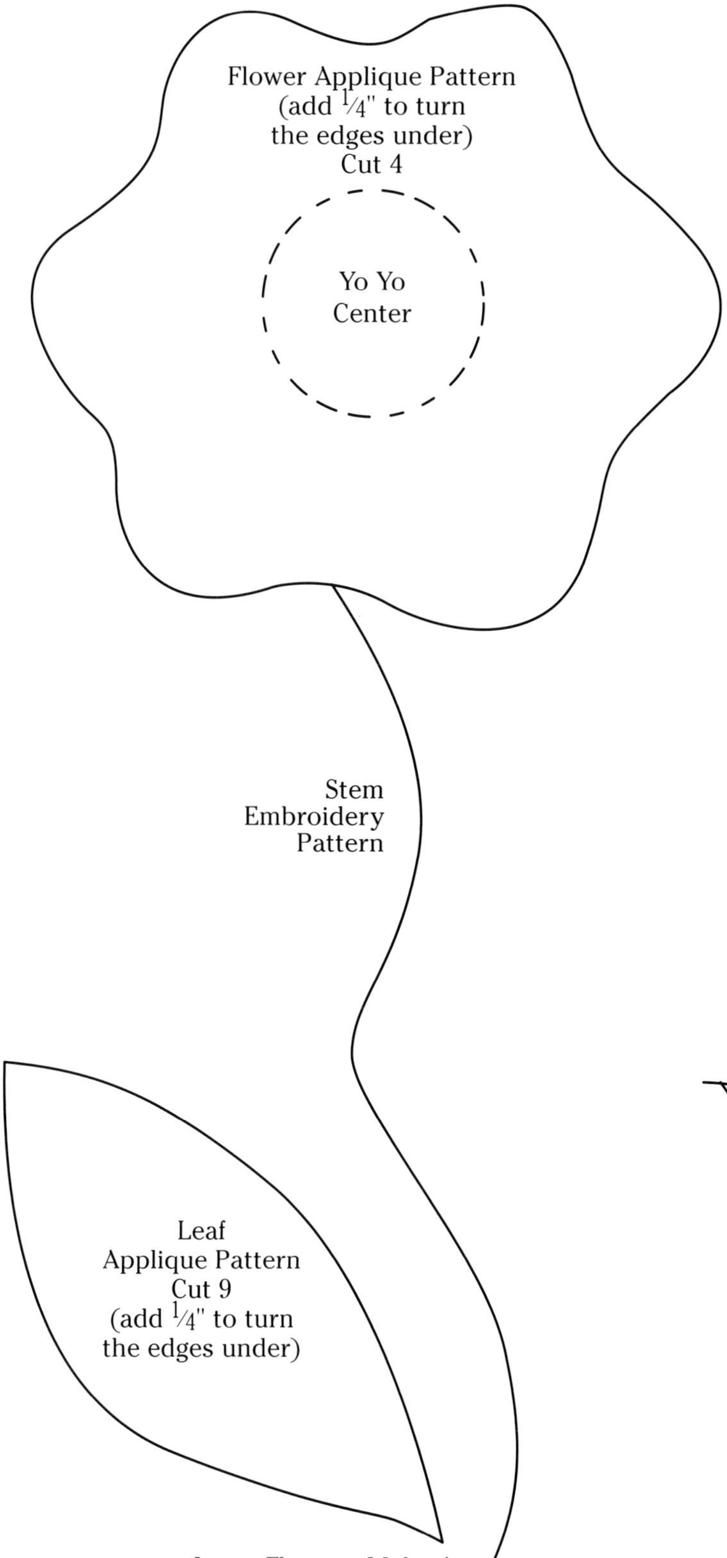

Applique:

Applique patterns

Flowers:
    Cut 2 Gold strips 2½" x 17".
    Sew 2 Gold strips together to make a piece 4½" x 17".
    Trace and cut out 4 applique flowers.
    Follow the Basic Applique instructions on page 28.
    Sew Brown yo-yos to the flower centers.

Large Leaves:
    Cut out 9 Black/Green leaves (6 Dark Green & 3 Light Green).
    Applique leaves next to the stems.

Yo-Yos:
    Cut 2 Brown strips 2½" x 14".
    Sew the strips together to make a piece 4½" x 14". Press.
    Cut 2 Green strips 2½" x 17½".
    Sew the strips together to make a piece 4½" x 17½". Press.
    Cut 5 Black/Green 3½" circles for yo-yo small flowers on the house.
    Cut 4 Brown 3½" diameter circles for yo-yo flower centers.
    Sew a Running stitch around the outer edge of each circle and gather into a yo-yo.
    Sew the Green yo-yos to the House block.

Embroidery:
    Stem stitch leaves and stems of appliqued flowers with Forest Green pearl cotton.
    Stem stitch leaves and stems of yo-yo flowers with Green pearl cotton.
    Stem stitch the rays of the sun on the Log Cabin block with Yellow pearl cotton.

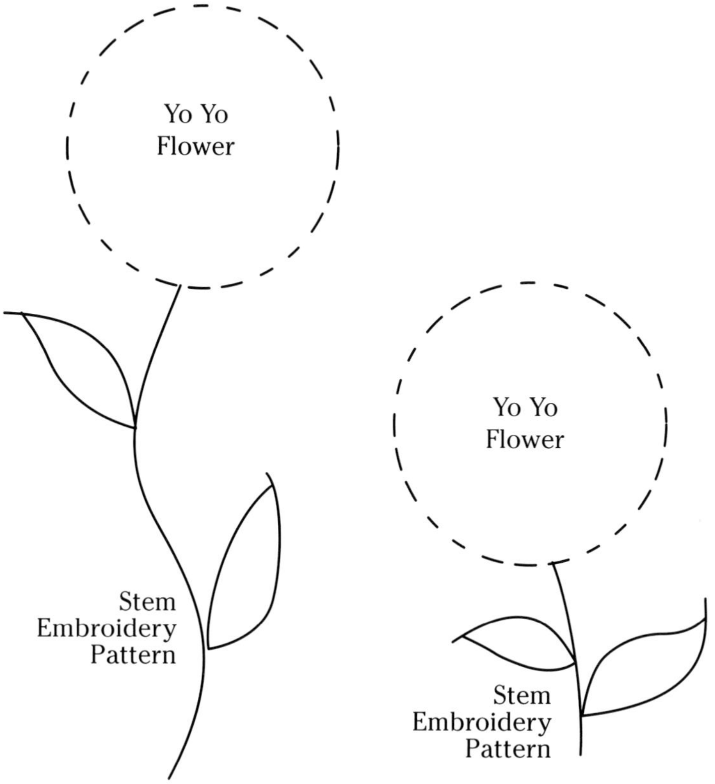

Flower Applique Pattern
(add ¼" to turn the edges under)
Cut 4

Yo Yo Center

Stem Embroidery Pattern

Leaf Applique Pattern
Cut 9
(add ¼" to turn the edges under)

Large Flower - Make 4

Yo Yo Flower

Yo Yo Flower

Stem Embroidery Pattern

Stem Embroidery Pattern

Small Flower - Make 5

Simply Strips & Squares

Prairie Paisley
photo on page 45

SIZE: 54" x 74"

YARDAGE:
We used a *Moda* "Prairie Paisley" by Minick & Simpson 'Jelly Roll' collection of 2½" fabric strips
  - we purchased 1 'Jelly Roll'
⅔ yard Blue (Light and Medium) OR 9 strips
½ yard Navy OR 6 strips
⅞ yard Ivory OR 12 strips
¼ yard Red OR 3 strips
½ yard Tan OR 7 strips

Border #1   Purchase ¼ yard Red
Border #2 & Binding Purchase 1¼ yards Blue
Backing   Purchase 3½ yards
Batting   Purchase 62" x 82"
Sewing machine, needle, thread

PREPARATION FOR BLOCKS
Sew all strips in preparation section together side by side.

Red-Tan Short Sections:
Sew a Red strip to a Tan strip to make 4½" x 44".
    Press. Make 3 sets.
Cut lengths into 27 sections 4½" x 4½".
    Set 5 sections aside for Row 6.

Blue-Tan Short Sections:
Sew a Light Blue strip to a Tan strip to make 4½" x 44".
    Press. Make 3 sets.
Cut 1 Light Blue strip 2½" x 27". Cut 1 Tan 2½" x 27".
    Sew strips together to make 4½" x 27". Press.
Cut lengths into 33 sections 4½" x 4½".
    Set 6 sections aside for Row 6.

Navy-Blue Long Section:
Sew a Navy strip to a Blue (Light or Medium) strip to make
    4½" x 44". Press. Make 5 sets.
Cut 1 Navy strip 2½" x 25½". Cut 1 Blue 2½" x 25½".
    Sew strips together to make 4½" x 25½". Press.
Cut lengths into 28 sections 4½" x 8½".

Ivory-Ivory Long Section:
Sew two Ivory strips together to make 4½" x 44".
    Press. Make 5 sets.
Cut 2 Ivory strips 2½" x 17".
    Sew strips together to make 4½" x 17". Press.
Cut lengths into 27 sections 4½" x 8½".

Tan-Ivory Short Sections:
Sew leftover Ivory and Tan strips to make at least
    4½" x 27". Press.
Cut lengths into 6 sections 4½" x 4½".

SEW BLOCKS:
For Block A1: Sew 21 Red-Tan short sections to the top of
    21 Navy-Blue long sections. Make 21.
For Block A2: Sew 6 Tan-Ivory short sections to the top of
    6 Navy-Blue long sections. Make 6.
For Block B: Sew 27 Tan-Blue short sections to the top of
    27 Ivory-Ivory long sections. Make 27.
Each block will measure 4½" x 12½" at this point.

Row 6:
Take Red-Tan and Tan-Blue short sections you set aside
    and arrange them following the Row 6 diagram.
Sew the blocks together. Press.

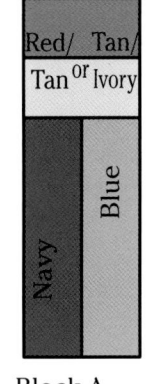

Block A
A1 - Make 22 with Red-Tan at the top.
A2 - Make 6 with Tan-Ivory at the top.

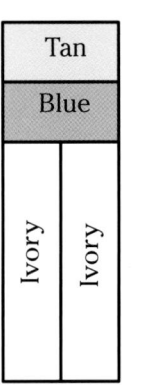

Block B
Make 27

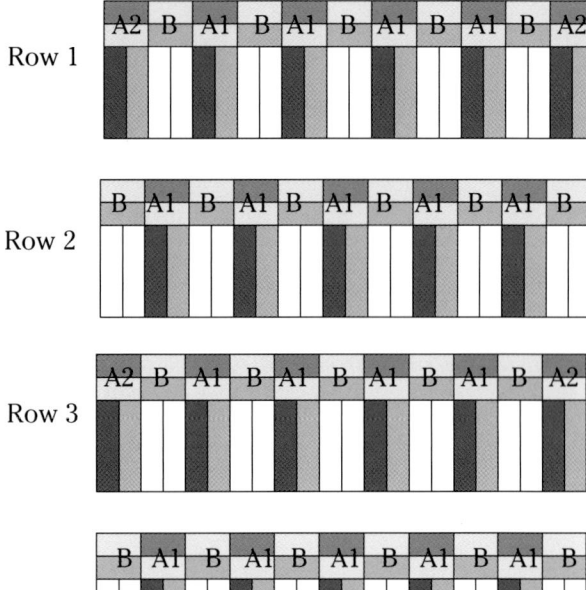

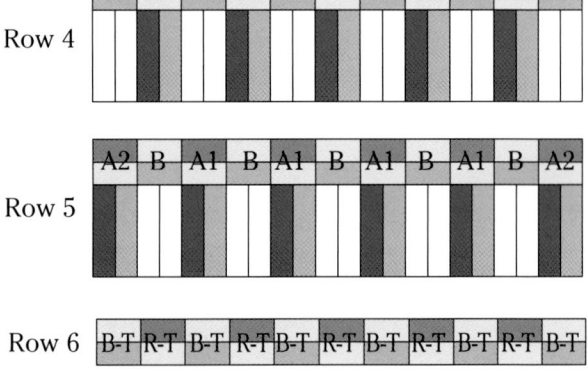

Prairie Paisley - Quilt Assembly Diagram

44 *Simply Strips & Squares*

ASSEMBLY:
Arrange all Blocks A and B on a work surface or table.
Refer to diagram for block placement and direction.
Sew blocks together in 5 rows, 11 blocks per row. Press.
Sew rows together. Press.
Sew row 6 to the quilt. Press.

Border #1:
Cut 1½" strips.
Sew strips together end to end.
Cut 2 strips 1½" x 64½" for sides.
Cut 2 strips 1½" x 46½" for top and bottom.
Sew side borders to the quilt.
Sew top and bottom borders to the quilt. Press.

Border #2:
Cut 4½" strips.
Sew strips together end to end.
Cut 2 strips 4½" x 66½" for sides.
Cut 2 strips 4½" x 54½" for top and bottom.
Sew side borders to the quilt.
Sew top and bottom borders to the quilt. Press.

FINISHING:
Quilting:
See Basic Instructions on pages 26 - 28.
Binding:
Cut seven 2½" strips.
Sew together end to end to equal 264".
See Binding Instructions, page 29.

Prairie Paisley

pieced by Donna Perrotta
quilted by Julie Lawson
In the tradition of the old string quilt, this wonderfully simple construction works into a stunningly beautiful quilt. More subtle than the usual red, white, and blue, this navy, ivory, and blue collection offers just a spark of red - enough to brighten the room without explosively intruding upon your decor. This inspiring design whispers "do me first" in the ear of every quilter and "take me home" to everyone who sees it.
instructions on page 44

Simply Strips & Squares 45

46 *Simply Strips & Squares*

'Through the Garden Gate

'Block of the Month'

A Morris Garden

pieced by Donna Hansen
quilted by Julie Lawson

Stroll past this white picket fence and pass through the garden gate into an elegant backyard garden. Trees and flowers welcome you on this sunny day with fragrant blossoms and soft breezes.

instructions on pages 38 - 43

Simply Strips & Squares

Baby and Toddler 'Swell' Quilts

pieced by Donna Hansen
quilted by Julie Lawson

Two for the Price of One!
Use one 'Jelly Roll' to make two colorful quilts. Begin by dividing the colored strips into "girl" colors, and "boy" colors, then sew the strips in simple blocks. Charming and simple.

instructions on pages 32 - 33

A 'Swell' Girl
Sassy reds combine with perky pinks in an attractively fresh departure from the usual pastel girl quilt. Hang it on the wall or cover a small dresser for a bright addition to your child's room decor.

A 'Swell' Boy
Snips and snails and puppy dog tails...little boys prefer the colors of the great outdoors. Decked out in greens and blues, this simple design is a great beginner project for a baby boy's room.

48   *Simply Strips & Squares*

'Swell' Simple Blocks Quilt

pieced by Donna Hansen
quilted by Julie Lawson

Flash back to the fifties and sixties with Swell prints and patterns brimming with memories of a simpler time. This simple pattern is a breeze to construct.

instructions on pages 30 - 31

Simply Strips & Squares 49

50 Simply Strips & Squares